ITSM LIBRARY

*it*SMF
THE IT SERVICE
MANAGEMENT FORUM

METRICS
for IT Service
Management

VHP

About the ITSM Library series

The publications in the ITSM Library cover best practice in IT Management and are published on behalf of itSMF Netherlands (itSMF-NL).

The IT Service Management Forum (itSMF) is the association for IT service organizations, and for customers of IT services. itSMF's goal is to promote innovation and support of IT management; suppliers and customers are equally represented within the itSMF. The Forum's main focus is exchange of peer knowledge and experience. Our authors are global experts.

The following publications are, or soon will be, available.

Introduction-, Foundations and Practitioners books
- Foundations of IT Service Management based on ITIL® / IT Service Management, an introduction - based on ITIL® (Arabic, Chinese, Danish, German, English, French, Italian, Japanese, Korean, Dutch, Portuguese, Russian, and Spanish)
- IT Services Procurement, an introduction based on ISPL (Dutch)
- Project Management based on PRINCE2™ 2005 Edition (Dutch, English, German)
- Practitioner Release & Control for IT Service Management, based on ITIL® (English)

IT Service Management - best practices
- IT Service Management - best practices, part 1 (Dutch)
- IT Service Management - best practices, part 2 (Dutch)
- IT Service Management - best practices, part 3 (Dutch)

Topics & Management instruments
- Metrics for IT Service Management (English)
- Six Sigma for IT Management (English)
- The RfP for IT Outsourcing - A Management Guide (Dutch)
- Service Agreements - A Management Guide (English)
- Frameworks for IT Management (English)

Pocket guides
- ISO/IEC 20000, a pocket guide (English, German, Italian, Spanish, formerly BS 15000 - a pocket guide)
- IT Services Procurement based on ISPL - a pocket guide (English)
- IT Governance - a pocket guide based on COBIT (English, German)
- IT Service CMM, a pocket guide (English)
- IT Service Management - a summary based on ITIL® (Dutch)
- IT Service Management from hell! (English)

For any further enquiries about ITSM Library, please visit www.itsmfbooks.nl, http://en.itsmportal.net/en/node/14063 or www.vanharen.net.

Metrics for
IT Service
Management

Van Haren
PUBLISHING

Colophon

Title:	Metrics for IT Service Management
A publication of:	itSMF-NL
Editorial team:	Peter Brooks (author) Jan van Bon (chief editor) Tieneke Verheijen (editor)
Publisher:	Van Haren Publishing, Zaltbommel, www.vanharen.net
ISBN-10: ISBN-13	90 77212 69 8 978-90-77212-69-1
Copyright	© itSMF 2006
Version:	First edition, first impression, April 2006 First edition, second impression, August 2006 First edition, third impression, December 2006
Design & Layout:	DTPresto grafisch ontwerp & layout, Zeewolde - NL
Printer:	Wilco, Amersfoort -NL

For any further enquiries about Van Haren Publishing, please send an e-mail to:
info@vanharen.net

The International itSMF organization, through its International Publications Executive Sub-Committee (IPESC), comprised of a council of members from global itSMF chapters has given its formal itSMF International endorsement to this book.

Foreword

Wherever Service Management is discussed around the globe the topic of Metrics soon follows. For those implementing or involved with IT service management a method of measuring results is fundamental.

Measurement within an organization can either be relatively subjective and informal or rigorously applied within the context of a formal standard or framework. However, regardless of the interpretation, one factor remains: the Metrics used must be relevant to the business objectives and the expected outcomes to be of any value.

I am pleased to say that this book will serve its readers well here. As the Chair for the itSMF International Publication committee (IPESC), I am very proud to officially add our Committee's formal endorsement of this publication.

The IPESC, through its council of members, their efforts and dedication create added value to the community of ITSM professionals, by endorsing the development of a common global library which supports a uniform understanding of ITSM best practices and knowledge.

Our endorsement process is a rigorous one, with stringent criteria that any ITSM-related publication must meet before it can be endorsed by the IPESC.

On behalf of the itSMF global community, I wish to thank the IPESC for their efforts and endorsement of this book.

I know that you will find it informative and a valuable addition to your ITSM library in support of your journey toward service excellence.

Sharon Taylor
Chair, International Publications Executive Committee
itSMF International

Contents

Acknowledgements

Following feedback from members, Metrics guidance has been high on the itSMF agenda for a long time. The fact that existing publications offered limited information has led to many requests from members for more detailed and practical guidance. The first publication in the ITSM Library to cover structured information on metrics was the pocket guide on CobiT ("IT Governance, a pocket guide based on CobiT"). This publication was developed with the intent to bring valuable information on Key Performace Indicators and Critical Success Factors for IT management processes to the field of IT Service Management. But it filled only part of the gap.

So when Peter Brooks approached us, we were delighted to have the opportunity to extend the information on metrics for IT Service Management. May 2005 we started the joint community project to document the common best practice in metrics guidance.

With his deep level of expertise, Peter Brooks took the role of author in the editorial project. Tieneke Verheijen acted as coordinating editor with responsibility for all the quality improvements we have delivered through a thorough review process. The project was run under the guidance of itSMF-NL's chief editor Jan van Bon who was responsible for the Project Management.

To ensure international knowledge and experience was reflected, a broad panel of experts was installed as the Review Team. The resulting editorial team formed a community, comprising the author, the editors, experts from the itSMF chapters and the itSMF International Publications Executive Sub-Committee (IPESC). This editorial team developed the scoping of the book by agreeing a Table of Contents.

The project was then turned over to the author and the editors: they gathered the best practices on metrics that they could find, using their own experiences, existing literature, many other sources and, of course, the web. In an intense and iterative peer review many other experiences were added by the Review Team. The result is this book: a thorough introduction to the field of metrics for IT Service Management, and a very valuable practical description of the best metrics we could find.

We owe Peter Brooks huge thanks for his never-ending enthusiasm and persistence, and his willingness to listen to the reviewers and seriously consider their issues. This has enabled us to develop a true common best practice on metrics for IT Service Management.

We also wish to thank our international Review Team, that has contributed their huge collective experience and knowledge. They provided encouragement, criticism and useful new ideas, to ensure that the book reflects the very best practice. Their input has really made a difference, especially in agreeing the structure and the initial Table of Contents, and adding very useful metrics to those already provided by Peter Brooks. But, most of all, they have ensured that difficult or unclear topics are explained in such a way as to provide an easy-to-read and practical book.

The Review Team consisted of:
- Rolf Akker - Atos Origin, the Netherlands
- Raul Assaf - Santa Monica Consulting, Argentina
- Bert Bouwmeester - Steenbok Automatisering, the Netherlands
- Gerard Brantjes sr. - Brantjes Advies Bureau, the Netherlands
- Alison Cartlidge - Xansa, United Kingdom
- Janaki Chakravarthy - Infosys Technologies Limited, India
- Young Sug Choi - itSMF, Korea
- Federico Corradi - Cogitek Consulting, itSMF Italy
- Bart den Dulk - Port of Rotterdam, the Netherlands
- John Groom - West-Groom Consulting, United Kingdom
- Ton van den Hoogen - Tot Z, the Netherlands
- Chris Jones - Ariston Strategic Consulting, Australia
- Henk de Jong - AEGON Nederland NV, the Netherlands
- Laurent Koelink - Quintica Consultants, the Netherlands
- Steve Mann - SM2 Ltd, United Kingdom
- Christian F. Nissen - Itilligence, Denmark
- Douglas Read - Pro-Attivo Limited, United Kingdom
- Ulrich Erik Redmann - Vattenfall Europe Information Services, Germany
- Adriaan van de Rijken - Quint Wellington Redwood, USA
- Parmjit Sangha - Direct Energy, Canada
- Russell Steyn - Foster Melliar, South Africa
- Antonio Valle - Abast Systems, Spain
- Wilfred Wah - IBM Global Services, Hong Kong

Their expert help has been invaluable.

We also want to thank the representatives of itSMF chapters in IPESC. They assessed the quality of the content of this itSMF publication, and the process by which it was produced, and have given their formal endorsement to this book in a unanimous vote. As a consequence this book is part of the core of the uniform understanding of ITSM knowledge and best practices, as it is used within the global itSMF organization. This is the best compliment we could get.

Given the desire for a broad consensus in the field of IT Service Management, new developments, additional material and other contributions from IT Service Management professionals are welcomed. They will be discussed by the editorial team and, where appropriate, incorporated into new editions. Any comments can be sent to the chief editor, email: jan.van.bon@itsmf.nl

Peter Brooks (FISM), Author
Tieneke Verheijen, Coordinating editor
Jan van Bon, Chief editor itSMF-NL

Introduction

IT service organizations are increasingly implementing Quality and IT Service Management standards. The IT Infrastructure Library (ITIL, ISO20000), Control Objectives for Information and Related Technology (COBIT), Six Sigma, enhanced Telecom Operations Map (eTOM) and Sarbanes Oxley (SOX) are emerging as some of the more popular standards in addressing IT Service Management, governance, quality and operational issues.

This book considers the design and implementation of metrics in service organizations using one or more of the frameworks mentioned above. It uses the ITIL process structure and many principles from the ITIL and ISO20000 (originally produced in the UK as BS15000) as a basis. It is a general guide to the use of metrics as a mechanism to control and steer IT service organizations.

Implementing IT Service Management as a series of interlocking processes - with 'process' strictly defined - enables a consistent view to be taken across the many disciplines that exist in a modern IT department.

This consistent view has been adopted as Best Practice by thousands of organizations across the world, with excellent results. The itSMF is an independent organization that champions the cause of IT Service Management in many countries by holding events, working to improve the practice advocated by ITIL through knowledge and experience sharing, whereby driving continuous refinement of the practice, and producing books such as this.

The ITIL processes all devote a section to possible metrics, giving an excellent starting framework for setting up metrics. For example, there is a chapter focusing on Key Performance Indicators (KPIs) in the ITIL Best Practice book 'Planning to Implement Service Management'. This guide deals specifically with the issue of setting up metrics in the context of IT Service Management frameworks, with a special focus on ITIL.

A major reason for writing this book is that many organizations have found it very difficult to use metrics properly. This book will deal with the causes of the difficulties to implementing metrics and will present workable solutions.

The book is a general guide to the design, implementation and use of metrics as a mechanism to control and steer IT service organizations. It also provides specific recommendations for applying metrics across the ITIL, ISO20000 and other processes, discussing the rationale of the recommendations. This enables an organization to implement the metrics as described directly as a first-pass solution that can be benchmarked against other organizations. But they can also be used as a starting point for customizing particular metrics.

Badly designed metrics can be actively harmful to an organization's proper functioning. Producing a set of metrics that avoids the pitfalls and delivers genuine value is not easy. This book will make that task much simpler and less error prone.

The recommended audience for this book is service managers, process owners, consultants, general IT management and anybody interested in mastering metrics of IT Service Management.

A worldwide review team of matter experts who have provided the benefit of many decades of collective IT and Service Management experience has extensively reviewed this book. You can rely on it as a guide to Best Practice in the field.

1   What are metrics all about?

A 'metric' is just another term for a measure. In IT, metrics have come to mean particular things to different people. Though this book is about metrics, it is important to remember why we use metrics. Simply measuring things for the sake of it is expensive and pointless. Metrics themselves are not an end. Metrics are an important part of the Management System that steers and controls IT in the desired direction. As we will see, Metrics must be designed in line with customer requirements, they must be benchmarked to ensure that they are achievable and they must be monitored to ensure that they keep within desired thresholds with action taken to correct any problems. They also are the target of the Continuous Service Improvement Programme (SIP), as processes and services are continuously improved, so are the metrics that measure them.

It is important to understand what the business' objectives are and ultimately arrange that all measuring, monitoring and control is aligned to attaining these objectives. This chapter discusses ways to ensure this.

1.1   Objectives

The aims, or the objectives, of using metrics in IT Service Management are:

1. to align business objectives with IT
- to provide accounting for IT processes and deliverables,
- to inform stakeholders of IT Service Management,
- to assist stakeholders in understanding IT performance and issues.

2. to help achieve compliance requirements for business operations
- to steer IT operations strategically,
- to help attain ISO20000, COBIT or other certifications,
- to achieve Critical Success Factors (CSFs) - see later discussion section 1.3 and 10.2,
- to minimize interruption of the business.

3. to drive operational excellence of IT strategically
- to measure IT & process performance,
- to control IT Service Management processes,
- to manage IT tactically,
- to maximize IT productivity and performance,
- to prove the value creation of the IT organization.

In short, to steer the particular area being measured in the right direction.

1.2   Business & IT Alignment

ITIL is designed to align IT with business needs, as are other Quality Management initiatives, such as COBIT and Six Sigma. Common to all these is a need to understand the business goals, the needs of the various stakeholders and what part IT plays in assisting with achieving those goals and delivering services to those needs.

1.2.1 Metrics as Management Information

The business has to understand how well its business processes are performing. IT plays an important role in three ways to assist with this.

Firstly, IT nowadays often is responsible for providing accounting, logistical and other direct services to business processes. Accordingly, the measures are provided in management reports to the various business units - for example SAP reports on sales, provided to the Sales team.

Secondly, IT provides services to business processes documented in the Service Catalogue, with the detail of delivery defined in the various SLAs set up between the Service Level Manager and business customers. These measures are shown as exception reports to Key Performance Indicators (KPIs) based on negotiated SLAs. Trends in these reports show how IT is improving its ability to provide services to a high standard.

Thirdly, IT itself is an important business process, a business contingency plan without a substantial section on IT service continuity is rare! Thus, IT reports on the operation of IT processes are part of the management information required by the business. These metrics form the bulk of the discussion in this book. They're based on the measurement of IT Service Management process operation.

This information is, however, business information, so detailed technical metrics are not appropriate. Rather the condensed results of measurement of IT processes can be presented in business terms. Ultimately business measures are monetary measures so the aim of IT is eventually to provide Return on Investment (ROI), Return on Capital Employed (ROCE), Economic Value Added (EVA) or any other expression.

Before this can be done, however, IT Financial Management, in ITIL terms, must have reached a high level of maturity. Until then, measures of process efficiency, along with KPIs against SLAs provide the most complete picture of IT's services to the business.

Once clear and relevant metrics have been designed, it is important that they are presented clearly. Various ways of achieving this are discussed below, such as 'balanced scorecard', 'traffic light' and 'dashboard' systems. Different reporting methods and different sets of metrics will be appropriate for different audiences. The naming of metrics is also important so that, if a metric is changed from one reporting period to another this is made clear.

If processes are not implemented in a consistent, repeatable manner, the metrics produced by them will be unreliable. It is important, as ISO20000 emphasizes, for there to be a sound Management System in place with sufficient maturity and process management to be part of an organization's way of doing things for metrics to provide useful measurement.

1.2.2 Metrics for Management Control

When something in business is measured, particularly when this measure is made the responsibility of a manager or a team of people, the behavior of the people measured changes.

If the metrics are well designed and the objectives of the metrics are in line with business requirements, this behavior will tend to be in line with these business requirements. In other words, a well designed and measured metric is a method of control. If a metric is not well designed, is not in line with actual business requirements or is not measured correctly then this 'control' can drive behavior in the opposite direction and harm the operation of the business.

There are many examples of this. Just one will suffice to show the problem. In the UK, the government decided that the length of time patients had to wait for operations was a useful metric. To measure this it set targets to reduce the length of waiting lists. The result was exactly the behavior the government had requested. The waiting lists got shorter and the targets were met. However patients were actually waiting just as long for their operations as before. Hospital administrators were not allowing patients to be entered onto the waiting list until their operation had been scheduled to a time within the target waiting time. Thus, a second, informal, waiting list came into being. On it were those waiting to be allowed onto the waiting list!

This example is a good one for a few reasons. One is that it shows the ingenuity of people in working to produce exactly what is asked for, and measured, rather than what is actually sought, the *letter* of the law rather than the *spirit* of the law. It also shows that a measure must be designed to actually measure what is important. In this case a waiting list was measured. However, it would have been more appropriate, but quite possible more difficult, to measure patient referral dates against patient operation dates. So, the design of the measure is important. The final problem was that the process itself was not measured, so when a new process (the informal waiting list for the waiting list) was invented by hospital administrators, it was not visible to the government auditors.

Another problem many organizations have met is indecision. If metrics have been badly designed, they have to be changed, of course. However, if they are changed to try to address the immediate problem, rather than carefully designed, the new metrics may prove almost as bad. This will then mean that they have to be changed again. If metrics are changed every few months there is no reason for anybody to work hard to achieve them. People soon work out that they only have to wait for the change, and there will be a new period of uncertainty in which there is no effective metric and hence no effective management control. An organization under the effect of constantly changing metrics is likely to be worse off than one with no metrics at all.

We are all happy to work for goals that we think have a reasonable chance of attaining. We also work better if we are given recognition, and sometimes even praise, when we do a job well. If we are asked to do an impossible job, we know that we can only be blamed for not managing to do it. The natural human response to this is to give up and simply go through the motions of trying. Metrics must be set to be perceived as achievable and make business sense so as to encourage positive change of behaviour.

The moral of this is that metrics must be achievable and recognition and praise must be given to those who achieve and excel in over-achieving against the metrics.

The various process metrics enable the IT organization as a whole to measure the effectiveness of managers in implementing, improving and maintaining the quality of the delivery in their areas of responsibility.

1.2.3 Metric integration & Reporting

Metrics do involve detailed measures of technical matters. This is unavoidable. However, once the key metrics have been set, these can be reported using the 'traffic light' or 'dashboard' methods, discussed in detail in chapter 7. This method allows a 'drill-down' into the detail to occur when a problem is isolated at the top level.

If the metrics for different processes are designed in a similar way, the management of these processes can be compared with each other. Though the Change Management Process is a very different thing from the Availability Management Process the management, maturity and effectiveness of these two processes can be compared by having similarly structured integrated metrics, particularly if these metrics include an accurate measure of customer satisfaction, in which the 'customer' is defined as the main beneficiary from the output of the process.

For example: if Availability Management has a score of 8.5 on the weighted sum of its ten metrics and Change Management has a score of 10.8 on its metrics, we can see that Availability Management is less in control of its processes than Change Management, even though the processes themselves are quite different.

How these scores are set and exactly what they might mean will be the subject of chapter 7.

1.2.4 Metrics aligned to stakeholders

Communication is a vital part of IT Service Management. If stakeholders are being informed by metrics, they can contribute to the success of the enterprise by supporting the openness and transparency, and by seeing the improvement. Each section below discusses the needs of particular stakeholders and how they fit into the customer relationship diagram (figure 6.1).

This enables appropriate communication of metrics, their results and what these results mean in terms of delivery of services to stakeholders. Stakeholders need to be an integral part of IT definition and satisfied with the results they see from their active involvement.

Communication is a two-way process so it is important to integrate requirements from the various stakeholders and use their involvement throughout to improve service delivery and process operation.

For this to be handled properly, it is important that it is dealt with using a carefully constructed communication plan, using stakeholders to assist in its construction and review.

Customer

In this book, by using the word 'customer', we usually mean the purchaser of a service, be it internal or external. In this section we refer to the end customer of the business. Ultimately all business effort ought to be directed towards the end customer. IT provides a support function for the business processes, but sometimes the IT contribution is experienced by the business, end customer (the ultimate customer) as well.

In these cases, to be sure that we have contributed effectively to the business, the business must measure the satisfaction of all end customers. This measurement must, however, be handled sensitively. If we demand surveys too frequently from customers, this activity itself will become a negative factor to them. If we don't solicit advice on how well we are doing often enough, there is a danger of not being aware of service incidents for long enough for them to impact our customer satisfaction seriously.

User

Since users do not negotiate the terms of their service and do not pay for it, they are not direct customers of IT. However, as stakeholders, their satisfaction with the service is vital. If users are not satisfied as they are being supplied with poor quality services, eventually our customers will not be satisfied.

Employee

Employees within IT have the responsibility to deliver service processes. IT, in return, has the responsibility to supply good working conditions with fair evaluation and reward. If employees are not satisfied the service levels provided will be less than they ought to be, no matter how well defined the metrics are. Thus, it is an imperative of IT management to measure staff morale and be sensitive to changes that might impact it negatively.

Employees are happier when they feel recognized as a stakeholder. Also, they need to be able to identify with their employer, out of positive respect for the business, and approval of the processes. Communicating metrics to employees clearly and openly, enables them to understand where IT is doing well and where there are issues that require further effort. Effective communication enables employees to address issues and to find an inspiration to further effort.

Board

Senior management and the Board have a particular need, as stakeholders. In order for the business to thrive, they require advance warning of any potentially serious incidents so that urgent corrective actions can be taken. An open and transparent communication with the Board can help as these incidents can be identified before they become too serious to remedy.

Good news is also important to the Board. It can be communicated both within and outside the company to enhance its reputation. The attainment of ISO20000, for example, ought to be an opportunity for the Board to report the achievement with pride.

Other stakeholders like government and shareholders

Though these stakeholders are important to the business, the correct communication to them is the Board's responsibility. If IT has messages that can reassure or warn such stakeholders it is important that they are communicated first to the Board. In this way, the Board can decide on the appropriate channel and method of communication.

1.3   Why Metrics are not SLAs

The agreement between the business organization, the customer, and IT is negotiated by the Service Level Manager and results in a set of defined Service Level Agreements (SLAs). These SLAs define what service levels IT agrees to provide.

These SLAs are used by the Service Level Manager to define the Operational Level Agreements (OLAs) and, where third parties are involved, the Underpinning Contracts (UC) that enable the service to be delivered.

The Critical Success Factors (CSFs) for IT are defined by the OLAs - if you look at it from a bottom-up point of view. If an OLA is met then the relevant CSF will be satisfied - if the match between them is good. Actually OLAs are derived from SLAs which rely on CSFs, so are broader in scope than a particular OLA may be. For a member of the organization, though, the CSF can be seen as the goal of the OLA.

CSFs are the service delivery measures that must be met to satisfy the SLAs. Each CSF can then be used to define a Key Performance Indicator (KPI) that is a measure of whether the CSF is being delivered.

Thus the entire chain:

Customer Requirement ⋯⋗ **SLA** ⋯⋗ **OLA/UC** ⋯⋗ **CSF** ⋯⋗ **KPI** ⋯⋗ **Monthly Report**

is driven directly by the customer requirements and the KPIs can be measured and reported back to the customer to show how effectively the IT organization is meeting the agreed service levels.

1.4   Metrics and KPIs

As we see above, the KPI provides a customer facing metric that measures the success with the SLAs defined with the customer.

This enables IT management to know each month whether it is doing well or not. This is too late to do anything about it! It is no good having a petrol gauge in your car that tells you that the tank is empty. You need one to tell you how full the tank is so that you can fill up before it becomes a problem.

In just the same way, IT management must have measures that show how the organization is operating daily or weekly so that corrections can be made before SLAs are compromised.

This is where process metrics come in to play. The ITIL approach to IT Service Management defines delivery in terms of services to customers. This is why the KPI is the proper measure of service delivery. However, ITIL also defines the operation of the various parts of IT in terms of processes. Each of these processes can be seen as an engine that takes certain input and processes it into output, as figure 1.1 points out.

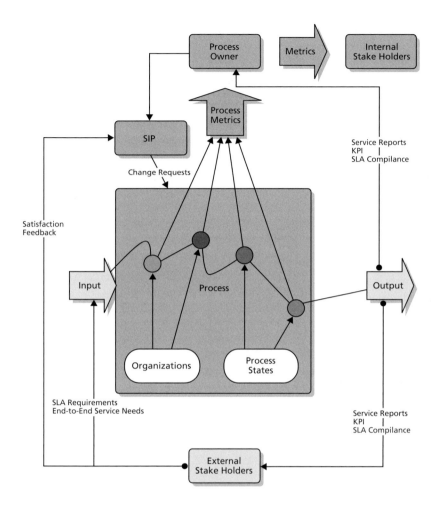

Figure 1.1: General Process Schematic

The process flow between Organizations and/or Process States is shown along with the contribution to Metrics. This diagram also shows the alignment between this process and both internal and external stakeholders. *Dark gray* represents processes and organizations internal to IT whilst *pale gray* represents external connections and organizations.

As can be seen, for the process owner to control the working of the process to deliver its goals, KPIs are defined for the process. These are measured daily or hourly and triggers on thresholds decide escalations to enable corrective actions.

Each process, however, working with the other ITIL processes, must be managed by metrics that can be reported to IT management and to other stakeholders, to contrast the process operation of the different IT processes. The careful selection and measurement of the process metrics as shown enables the management of the process, as a process, the measurement of the process owner and, where relevant, the process team. These metrics include some of the KPIs used by the process owner. He, however, is likely to use a larger set of metrics, giving more detail of day-to-day changes in process delivery, thus providing more hands-on management.

1.5 Metrics and Benchmarking

Over a longer period of time it is possible to measure previous results of metrics and compare one month or year to previous months and years. These comparisons can be used to set performance improvement goals.

There are two problems with this. Firstly, when metrics are introduced, it is not clear what an acceptable or ideal level of performance might be. In order to establish this, it is necessary to produce an initial base level or 'benchmark'. This is often done by running the metrics for two or three periods and then taking the values produced as a 'benchmark' of the minimum requirement and working from there.

The second problem is knowing whether this benchmark compares well or badly with other organizations. If your metrics are uniquely set for your organization this will be an impossible question to answer! Nobody else uses your metrics, so only you know what values are possible.

There are two approaches to resolving this. Some research organizations have produced lists of standard metrics with average results across a number of organizations. If you measure these same standard metrics then these figures can be used to identify how your organization sits relative to the average.

The other approach is to use either a standard set of metrics, or a set modified from a standard set, such as those in this book. Then it is possible to compare your metrics directly with other organizations using the same, or very similar, metrics.

A hybrid approach is also possible. If you implement your own metrics, but also measure two or three of the published research metrics, then benchmarking the research metrics can give an external view, giving an insight into how well the processes work.

> If, for example, the research metrics show your organization to be between 95 per cent and 115 per cent against the average, then the other metric goals can be scaled to fit within the same range. At some future time, if your own metrics are, say, 120 per cent to 130 against this benchmark then it can be reasonably assumed that you are at approximately that level relative to the organizations in the benchmark.

Using the method presented in this book of a reasonably standard set of metrics across all processes allows a third approach. It is possible to benchmark your processes against each other. ITIL is usually implemented in phases, so, if your weighted goals for a well established process, say Change Management, are achieved with an average of 130 per cent, then the benchmark goals for a new process can be set initially to give a weighted average result of, say, 80 per cent. This way process improvement over time can be measured to see how long this new process takes to equal the level of Change Management.

2   Why Metrics?

> *Cheshire Puss - she began, rather timidly, as she did not at all know whether it would like the name: however, it only grinned a little wider.*
> *Come, it's pleased so far - thought Alice, and she went on. - Would you tell me, please, which way I ought to go from here?*
> *That depends a good deal on where you want to get to - said the Cat.*
> *I don't much care where - said Alice.*
> *Then it doesn't matter which way you go - said the Cat.*
> *So long as I get somewhere - Alice added as an explanation.*
> *Oh, you're sure to do that - said the Cat - if you only walk long enough.*
>
> *Alice in Wonderland, Lewis Carroll*

We rely on metrics every day for many of the things we do. We simply do not think of them in quite that way! It is important to put metrics into perspective because there is a danger of being carried away. If you know what you want to do, or where you need to go, then you can decide what you need to measure to know how you are doing your way to get there and how it will help you. If you are given a machine with many different instruments, there is a temptation to find the instruments themselves exciting rather than what that machine is really useful for.

As with Alice, if we do not care where we are going it does not matter what we measure. If we do not measure where we are going then we are sure to get somewhere. But probably not where we would like to be!

2.1   Metrics as an instrument

The speedometer in a car or aircraft generates metrics; it provides a measure of how fast the driver is going. He will be aware when he's driving too fast, because he knows the maximum speed, and therefore knows what to do: brake or release the gas.

Before the days of very fast cars and speed traps, this was an unnecessary thing to measure. After all, you could tell how fast you were going from the wind in your hair and your speed around corners!

From even the earliest days a much more important instrument was the fuel gauge, particularly in aeroplanes. If you run out of fuel in a car you either have a long walk or, if you have come prepared, have to fill up from a spare can (a dangerous option). When you are flying your options are more limited so an accurate fuel gauge is that much more important.

In the language of metrics, having enough fuel to complete your journey is a Critical Success Factor (CSF) and the instruments, or metrics, used to measure it are your Key Performance Indicators (KPIs). If you are to concentrate on your driving or flying you need to keep these to a reasonably small number. So, as we have said, a fuel gauge is probably your top KPI.

An oil level indicator will be a close second since this can cause your engine to seize. These days, however, though these instruments are important, they are usually so reliable that we only need to know when it is time to fill up or when there is danger of overheating.

With these metrics, it is quite easy to see how the process model works. Consider the speedometer. The input will come from a transducer on the wheel. The output is the level of the indicator needle on the dial. The throughput, or the operation of the process itself, is the gearing (or now electronics) in the speedometer itself that translates the transducer input in so many thousands of turns into the output in so many kilometers per hour. The appropriate target levels of outcome will vary.

On a motorway they will be different from on a farm track. And the optimal outcome for the engine, as shown by the speedometer and the rev counter (tachometer), may not be appropriate because of legal speed restrictions.

The speedometer and odometer are less crucially important, to the functioning of the vehicle, but are more important to our trip. If we know the distance and at what time we are due to arrive, we can adjust our speed depending on the distance we see that we have come. If we have plenty of time in hand, we can even take breaks to ensure that we are alert enough to drive safely.

With all this in hand, our KPI, the matter that will decide if we arrive on time or not, might well be our ability to read the map properly, or a cell phone to help us navigate the last few kilometers to our destination with the help of landmarks and advice from those we are visiting. These are not instrumented (unless we have GPS in the car!) so it is less easy to measure unless things go wrong. This last point is another one to keep in mind with IT metrics!

2.2   Metrics as a control

The true control of a car is through the steering, the accelerator, brakes and gears. These allow us to control the car through minute changes to the road surface, unexpected hazards and other short-term contingencies. These are similar to day-to-day management in a company - or what is sometimes called 'micro-management', too much concern with the fine detail. This is not to say that the fine detail is not important, if you run over a log in the road and have a puncture, your journey time will certainly suffer!

The real long-term control comes from good planning, just like anything else! Properly selected metrics, with proper management, encourage properly defined activities that allow us to increase the certainty that we will arrive on time at the end of the journey. How often the car is serviced is one very long-term but important metric.

Good planning and map reading ensure that the journey does not have to be carried out at top speed with speeding, fast cornering and severe braking. All that will enable the journey to complete, but will also increase risk and make the journey uncomfortable for the passengers. They might decide to go by train next time!

Some instruments, the rev counter, for example, do not seem immediately valuable, some cars don't even have them. A sensitive driver, however, can use one to get the optimal performance from the car, without putting the engine under too much strain. If you were running a rally, points could be given to competitors who never redline the rev counter, but complete in the fastest time with the use of the minimum fuel. That calls for excellent driving, excellent planning and excellent navigation.

This long analogy applies pretty directly to IT metrics. In IT, there are KPIs that are so important that we just expect them to be done, like the fuel gauge being accurate! Other metrics are difficult to gather and only very sophisticated and mature IT organizations will need them to get optimal performance, like rev counters. Meanwhile most IT organizations will benefit greatly from using metrics to control the ride so that life is not all fire-fighting, sharp cornering, extreme braking, and the business, and people in IT, are comfortable enough to give of their best without unnecessary stress. It is important to remember that the measure is not enough to ensure the result - the activity must be managed in line with the metric - a well designed speedometer will not make you obey the speed limit!

Five different methods of coordinating organizational activities have been identified (Mintzberg). These can be likened to the various instrument options in the analogy, as table 2.1 shows.

Method of coordination	Analogy to driving a car
Direct Supervision	The supervisor instructs the driver to get the package to the customer by 17:00 this evening.
Mutual Adjustment	The drivers plan their breaks so that not all busses are unavailable at the same time.
Standardization of working practices	Drivers are taught to follow a pre-designed process.
Standardization of output	Drivers arrive at their destination with in time windows of ten minutes.
Standardization of capabilities	Drivers have advanced driving certificate.

Table 2.1 Five methods of coordinating organizational activities and their analogies to driving a car (after Mintzberg).

In the above examples, we see various ways of requesting desired results. Some require underlying metrics to be in place to help the measure - checking that all drivers have advanced driving certificates, for example. Others are ad hoc and need to be documented individually.

For IT management we can see that much of what occurs today is at the 'Direct Supervision' level. With the rise of ITIL, it is possible to put in place metrics that allow ITIL qualified people to implement standardized processes with standardized metrics. ISO20000 makes it clear that this works only if it is part of a coherent Management System.

2.3   Metrics and innovation

Metrics can only work if there is a process in place to be measured. Measuring how things happen without a process allows no consistent method of improvement, nor even a coherent way of discovering what prevented the metric occurring or how.

Much criticism of metrics comes from people who are opposed to processes rather than to metrics themselves. This is discussed more in section 10.3.1 on resistance. It is worth noting here that it is easy to agree to work according to a particular process and then carry on doing things just as before. Unless there are appropriate process metrics that will soon show that the process is not working.

Organizations that believe they have implemented processes but find that they appear to give little benefit may discover nothing has really changed when process metrics are established. For this reason, as well as the ones already mentioned, it makes sense to implement metrics at the same time as the processes are piloted, but this has often not been done!

There are a number of reasons for objecting to processes, and hence to metrics. One is simply that they are a change and most of us do not welcome change. Another is that they make a job boring as they force it to be done in a particular way each time. A further objection is that the measurement of process metrics exposes people to criticism and may endanger their jobs.

There is an element of truth to all the above objections, particularly if the reason for processes is not well communicated.

An analogy might help here. Riding a bicycle is a process. Once we learn how to do it, and those that have remember the wobbly start, the fear of falling off and the scraped knees that accompanied the learning, we no longer think about the detail. In fact, it has been pointed out that, if you think too carefully about what you are doing when riding a bicycle, you are likely to fall off! The important thing is that we then can concentrate on where we are going, what the view is like and the pleasure of being outdoors. If we never turn riding a bicycle into a well-known process, we will condemn ourselves to always finding it difficult, falling off and not enjoying the journey. We probably will not complete many journeys and certainly not many long ones.

So it is with IT Service Management or business processes. Once they are in place and working then it is possible to concentrate on the more interesting matters of introducing new things and fire fighting ceases to be a way of life. In an organization with good processes, people are free to innovate and give of their best in a calmer, more relaxed environment than in an organization that moves from crisis to crisis.

Yes, metrics do make problems visible and they have to be fixed. However, the object of the exercise is not to blame individuals, but to fix the process. It takes time for people to realize this, but it is vital for processes and their metrics to become accepted.

If metrics provide only the Red, Amber and Green traffic light reporting system, managers are tempted to look only for the Red metrics to see what the problems are. Reporting a Gold level where metrics are being not only met, but exceeded, is one possible way of enabling more positive celebration to happen, not just fault finding! It is, again, important for all to know, and for it to be emphasized, that process metrics are designed to enable processes to be improved, not find fault with people!

2.4   Costs

Measuring can cost a lot of money. One service management consultant was happy to save a company millions of pounds by closing down a department of over a hundred people who did nothing but produce reports. He found out all these reports were easier and cheaper to obtain from elsewhere in the organization.

One international organization sent out a monthly book of reports, called the 'Blue Book', because of its cover. One month, to test its importance, the management deliberately decided not to send out the report but wait for requests for it. Only one came. They were pleased to find that one person, out of the twenty who received the very expensive report, was interested in having it and asked why he wanted it. "My four year old daughter loves it because she can draw on the back of each page and it is very good paper", was his reply.

Reports are only worthwhile if they are used and they will only be used if they tell us something interesting. Metrics must be designed to measure important matters and reported in a clear and simple manner. For most managers, a one-page summary on a web site will be perfectly suitable to their needs, as long as any potential problems are communicated clearly. Hiding bad news in the notes at the back of reports might work for publicly listed companies, but it is not a sensible approach for IT!

Metrics that report on costs are important and, in the IT Service Management scheme, the responsibility of Financial Management. The level, or maturity, of the organization will determine at what level of cost metrics are produced. It is important not to report costs inaccurately. Waiting until a proper costing model has been agreed with the business by the Financial Management function through the SLA process would be better.

2.5   Benefits

This chapter ought to have made most of the benefits clear. To summarize:
- Metrics provide the instrumentation necessary to control an organization.
- Metrics make it easier to concentrate on the important matters.
- Well-presented metrics make it easy to spot danger in time to correct it.
- Metrics can improve morale in an organization.
- Metrics can stimulate healthy competition between process owners.
- Metrics help align IT with business goals.

3 Where to use metrics

IT Service Management software tools provide many possible metrics, most of which will be interesting to people in the relevant departments or running the relevant processes. If only these metrics are relied upon then the 'tail wags the dog'. The organization knows what the designer of the software thought it should know, not what business IT alignment demands.

For this reason it is important to start at the other end, design the processes for your organization, then design the metrics to measure them. After this, it is possible to decide how to implement them in software.

Since metrics are designed to allow an organization to control its destiny, somebody must be responsible for them. If two people are responsible for the same metric, neither person is, as the actions of one could prevent the other from achieving the desired result.

With process driven IT Service Management, whether you're using ITIL, Six Sigma, COBIT or all three, it is important to distinguish between individuals, organizations or departments, and processes. For a metric to be a successful control, it must be the responsibility of somebody, an individual, who has the authority necessary to influence the outcome of the metric. There is no point, as King Canute showed, of giving somebody responsibility for the tides in the sea, unless that person also is able to influence them!

For each metric, it is necessary to establish who the responsible person will be. Will it be a departmental manager or will it be a designated process owner who might not have any direct reports.

3.1 Departments

In IT Service Management, the most obvious two departmental entities that every organization has are the Service Desk (formerly known as the Help Desk) and the ICT Infrastructure Management team (formerly known as Operations). These two departments will have department heads responsible for metrics measuring their departmental efficiency, and for the processes for which their departments are responsible.

The Service Desk is often responsible for the Incident Management process. The manager of this department will then be the process owner responsible for the metrics.

Depending on the size and structure of the organization, there might be other departments in IT. These either carry ownership of one or more ITIL processes or provide services to these processes. It is important that appropriate metrics are established, in line with the top level processes but applying to the department's manager.

For example, consider an administrative department that provides reporting, of both ITIL process metrics and SLA compliance. It may have other duties as well, but metrics that test the accuracy and timeliness of production of these reports must be in place for the manager of this department. Such a department may also well have responsibility for the communication plan, an important plan that provides services to all other processes and must have its own measures of success.

3.2   Processes

Many processes don't have their own department to run the process, but rather run across many departments and organizations to deliver the end-to-end service. The person responsible for these is the process owner who must have authority to ensure that the process metrics are met, even with only influence management authority.

A good example of this is the Change Manager who is responsible for the Change Management process. One of the most important requirements for the implementation of IT Service Management along ITIL quality lines is an effective corporate sponsor. Change Management is always going to involve influence management, as so many different parties are involved. The Change Manager is responsible for final approval of changes, under advice. This is not always going to be a popular decision and there are opportunities for political, rather than business, considerations to come into play. The corporate sponsor is needed to provide the required support to the influence management of the Change Manager. This is possible if there is evidence that the Change Manager is doing a good job. Without metrics to prove it, this can be a matter of opinion and political undermining of the Change Manager becomes easier. Well chosen metrics for the Change Management process can help identifying organizational areas that are not as cooperative as they could be. Working with them to iron out any process difficulties can be made considerably easier by a strong executive sponsor.

It is worth repeating one point. People are very sensitive to criticism, real or imagined. Poorly performing processes, identified by metrics are an opportunity for improvement. They are not supposed to be an attack on people! It is important that this point is emphasized in communications.

4 Who should use metrics

The value of metrics will only be realized if they are actually used. Metrics are a form of communication and, like all communication, must be planned and delivered in a manner suitable to the audience. For this to be successful it is necessary to understand the different needs of users, or consumers of metrics.

Those receiving metrics also need to be aware of the purpose and proper use of the metrics. There is a danger that metrics will be looked at briefly to see what red items there are, so that these can be used as a stick to beat the relevant process owner or department. This approach, though sadly very common, is not helpful. Clearly red items are important and must be dealt with urgently by those responsible. But long-term trends and decisions for the future to avoid such situations are more important than simple fire fighting about the results from the previous period. Process owners receive metrics to help them manage the process because they are responsible for the process. Other managers will receive the metrics to assist with their own processes and so will be users of the metrics even though they are not actually responsible for them.

When implementing metrics consider a period of training or awareness raising before sending out the metric reports. This may need following up with discussions of future direction, benchmarks, goals and the Continuous Service Improvement Programme (SIP).

The level of detail carried in metrics determines how usable they are. Too many metrics will take too long to understand and are likely to be reduced to the 'red light' view described above. On the other hand, you can miss important trends if there is too little detail. This book aims at balancing these two extremes by proposing small understandable sets of metrics designed to capture the vital functions of the process.

4.1 Management

Business and IT management share the task of steering IT functioning towards optimal alignment with business needs. This is a never-ending job as it is the nature of business for requirements to change frequently, often in unexpected ways. Metrics, possibly as part of the framework of the Balanced Scorecard or other Business initiative, help provide measures of direction and levers for management control.

Metrics, by their very nature, can only provide information of what has occurred. It's important to make sure that what happens next is in line with what's required.

The most direct measure that business management has of IT services is the published performance against SLAs. Internal IT metrics showing how the various processes are performing are only an adjunct to this. Usually, when things are going well and SLA violations are infrequent making little impact to business function, there is no need for business management to be too concerned with internal functioning, unless there is an awareness of impending change to the business environment!

IT may be delivering services within agreed service levels but at high internal cost and stress. This is not sustainable in the long term. Alternatively the delivery might be coping well with current workloads but not have the capacity to ramp up to step-changes in requirements. A major merger might transform IT from an effective unit to helpless delivery failure, if it's not planned properly in advance. Knowing how IT is functioning from a consideration of the process metrics enables such planning with a proper knowledge of current capacity and issues.

Finally, SLAs can be set too tightly for actual business requirements. If the business negotiator has more authority or more experience in negotiating, the Service Level Manager may concede to unrealistic requests. Even without this, circumstances change and an appropriate SLA for one size of organization might be unrealistic for another. In reality, to maintain SLAs, they need to be under review and negotiation to ensure sensible alignment. Process metrics add an important 'reality check' for the Service Level Manager to show the actual cost (even if in terms of effort and resource usage and not in terms of money directly) of decisions reached on service levels. This gives business management the opportunity to revise decisions that provide small incremental benefit to business function whilst generating high IT overhead.

As mentioned in the introduction, to achieve the above aims of communication to management it is important for management to understand the process metrics and how they relate to financial cost. They must also understand less tangible, but still important, factors such as morale in IT or staff turnover that despite being difficult to measure still have substantial impact on service delivery.

4.2   Process managers

Process managers see lower level metrics and so have a better grasp of why trends in the KPIs are as they are. If there are to be any red items on the regular reports then the Process manager should be aware of this some time before the reports are available to IT and business management. This means supplying an explanation for the items along with corrective actions already in place.

Over time, though, dealing with red items should not be the priority. For the process manager, it is more important to be aware of trends that reveal possible dangers in the medium term future. The effort put into altering capacity or modifying process operation in order to anticipate and defuse dangerous future scenarios flagged by metric trends is far less than is required to deal with crisis situations when they arrive.

Process managers have a responsibility for running their own processes. However, they also have a wider business responsibility to inculcating a process-orientated culture.

This means that old-fashioned IT practices rewarding fire fighters for daring feats of bravery in saving the day at the last minute rather than reserving rewards for those that prevent the conflagration in the first place. This culture is quite deeply entrenched in many organizations and difficult to remedy.

Conspicuous celebration of steps taken and money saved by actions taken to defuse possible future crises helps. Well-publicized post-mortems of major crises with an emphasis on learning how to avoid them in future also play a role. The day-to-day communication of process, rather than exception, orientated operation values must be the constant background to slowly move the organization away from previous practices.

Though this is difficult, process managers must also take seriously the need to identify trends that show over-capacity and high over-heads brought about by efficiency changes or reduced demands from the business. Over the long term, process managers ought to be able to improve their processes, in order to deliver more with fewer resources. This is difficult as organizational culture can also reward those in charge of many staff over those who manage to deliver great value with few.

4.3 Staff

The change of organizational culture spoken about in the previous section is most important when applied to IT staff.

All members of IT need to understand what the process metrics, KPIs and SLAs are. Not just in general, but specifically how they apply to their own part of the organization and the processes for which they have some responsibility.

Ideally Human Resources will have re-designed job descriptions and performance evaluations, so that performance is expected, then measured and rewarded against achievement of the appropriate metrics.

The communication of exactly what metrics mean, what behavior they will reward and how achievement will be rewarded is important and continuous. Weekly or monthly staff meetings must focus on relative performance of the various processes and reward those exceeding targets. Just as factory floors now have graphs showing current performance metrics, so should IT departments show ownership of the metrics appropriate to them by having them prominently visible, to remind everybody what the goals are.

The area where front-line staff can provide the most valuable contribution is to the Continuous Service Improvement Programme (SIP). People working every day to deliver services using processes are in the best position to see how they can be improved. Such advice should be sought and effective suggestions handsomely rewarded. After all, it is much better to improve service delivery to end-users by a process improvement than by investing in more people, computers or other resources!

When performance falls below ideal levels, giving red light items on KPIs or process metrics, it is important to prevent recurrence by encouraging staff to suggest methods for improvement. It is important, in addition, not to see such problems as reasons to blame individuals, but rather as opportunities to find ways of future improvement.

It is also worth discussing future changes to metrics including staff in the delivery teams. Knowing directly what day-to-day problems there are enables them to visualize the effect of such changes and, with luck, avert unrealistic requests. Alternatively, suggestions to how to meet such challenges can be made in a collaborative environment rather than leading to resentment and resistance when they appear to be forced on departments from above, without a clear understanding of the likely impact.

It is a fact of all of us that we feel and perform better with less stress, when we have more control over our future. Staff who are properly engaged in the metrics setting and negotiation process will feel more of a responsibility to do well when measured against them. Intangible as such changes to morale may seem, they do most certainly deliver to the bottom line!

5 How to use metrics

5.1 Timing

How often you measure something affects what you will see. Metrics are often reported daily, monthly, weekly, quarterly or annually. It is important to ensure that the appropriate time interval is used.

It would be a mistake to make strategic business decisions from a daily report - it might just be an anomaly.

Similarly, an annual report of metrics will help give a strategic view of what actions need to be taken to improve things, but it would not be appropriate to decide on what tactical decisions the Service Desk should take next week.

As well as how often a metric is measured, it is important to realize that many metrics measure the time between status codes. How long it takes a problem record to move from 'created' to 'closed' for example. It is important to realize that this can only be measured when the status changes. If the status remains the same between two time periods then you have no additional metric information. You can only measure when something (usually a process) actually changes.

5.2 Measuring

In order to understand your business you need to measure it. In business terms there are some clear and concrete measures that are common across many businesses:
- Revenue
- Profit
- Volume of sales
- Market share
- ROI
- Manufacturing output
- Inventory levels

Some of these measures can be applied to IT processes. The better the alignment between business and IT, the easier this match can be made.

As usual, the danger is measuring things that are easy to measure rather than things that tell you something important about the business. It is easy to measure the number of items sold in a department store, but that measure gives equal weight to selling a packet of sweets or a washing machine so has very limited applicability. In IT, things are not so tangible as washing machines so it is more difficult to be sure that a measure does make sense.

Figure 5.1 shows how processes run through different organizations and produce an overall input and output. The coloured circles represent stages the process goes through. You can only measure something when it changes and so it is possible for the various organizations involved in a process to measure when a particular action or task in the overall process becomes their responsibility.

If we consider the *darkest gray* circle as a department responsible for performing a credit check on customers, then the overall process might be order processing. The credit department can measure when an order comes in and when it is passed to the next department as cleared or refused. This is a useful measure to Credit Control but might be less interesting to the process owner. Not all orders may go through Credit Control, small orders might be approved through a simpler mechanism. From the point of view of the process owner it is the approval stage that matters, how long it takes, how many errors there are in the process and so forth.

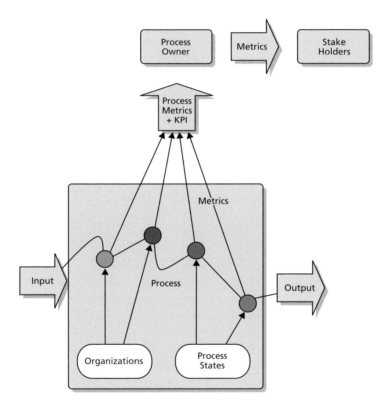

Figure 5.1 General Process Schematic; Metrics can only measure process state changes. Proper Process Definition is vital to meaningful metrics.

These different views are the reason we often look at this figure as a series of process states. An order moves from the 'state' of being 'not approved for credit' to 'credit approval' to 'approved for credit'. We can use this to measure the various relevant factors in this part of the process. Simply examine all orders that are in the state 'credit approval' and decide what other factors are interesting, for example:
• Order size
• Person or department processing the order
• Ultimate credit worthiness of the customer

The question we are really asking is "What is important for us to know about what happens to orders when the credit rating of the customer is being checked?". This business question focuses our mind on relevant business results.

In terms of an IT process the same thing occurs. We define process states and then, for each of them, decide what is important to achieving the desired process goal within the SLA.

Something important becomes clear now. The process states were quite clearly tied to a business process (and indeed a department as well) in the example of Credit Control. In IT the decision of where exactly to put a process state is often a lot less obvious. If a process state covers two sub-processes then neither of the two can be distinguished in a measure. Without careful process definitions our results can end up being meaningless or, worse, misleading.

It's important to notice as well that the transition from one state to another appears immediate in a diagram like figure 5.1. In real life this may not be the case at all. If an order is a paper copy it could take several hours for an order that has been 'credit approved' to move to the next state of order processing, because the order has to be physically collected and delivered to the next person. Even in electronic systems there can be delays, particularly if something is moved to the wrong person and then has to be rerouted to the correct one.

5.3   Controlling

Once you have a measure in place you can start to control the measured part of the process. You can identify who is responsible for a particular process state or transition between processes. Then it is possible to benchmark the sub-process either by watching the measure for one or two time-periods to get a feeling for normal activity, or by comparing it to a similar process elsewhere in the organization, or in another organization.

Once a benchmark is in place it is possible to negotiate with the sub-process owner to identify improvement goals. Timing information also allows the overall process owner to identify which states consume the most time and resources in the overall process flow. These can be identified as 'quick wins' sub-processes that can be improved with the greatest effect on the overall process time.

One important factor to remember here so as to get an accurate result is that not all states are equal. In the process state diagram shown by figure 5.2 we can see alternative routes.

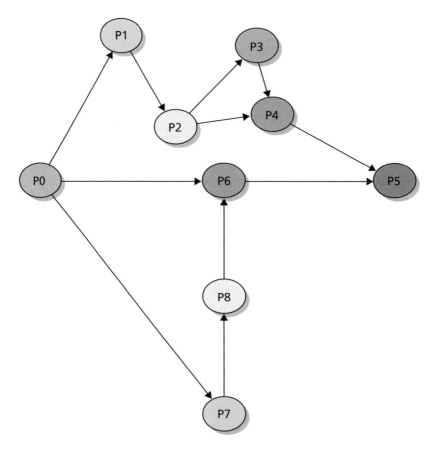

Figure 5.2 Process state diagram; The different grayscales represent the steps from the start and end of the process. The diagram shows legal state transitions.

This is not uncommon. It simply means that at the start of the process, P0, there are three possible options: P1, P6 or P7, which lead to the various alternatives. They all end up at the end process state of P5, so it would be possible to measure the time P0 -> P5, and it might be a useful control. However, particularly if processes P3, P7 and P8 are controlled by other parts of the organization, there is a danger that it will be difficult to find out why there is poor timing for this measure.

If P0 -> P5 represents an important part of the process delivering to an SLA then it is a legitimate metric to measure. However, to control the process, the process owner needs to have separate measures for the different branches to understand what proportion they contribute in terms of volume and delay. It might be, for example, that ninety per cent of the process traffic goes through the route P0 -> P6 -> P5, but all cases where there was a danger of not meeting the SLA went through the route P0 -> P1 -> P3 -> P4 -> P5. Huge improvement in the control of the overall process would be made by improving or redesigning the more complex top route. It would not be worth spending time on the high volume route until the complex one has been improved substantially.

5.4 Steering

It is all very well to control something. In the analogy with driving a car, if you are supposed to get to Amsterdam by nightfall you'll get no prizes for being in control of the car all day but end up in Paris!

This makes clear that, to steer a process you need to understand where you wish to go. In the business example of Credit Control, you may wish to keep bad debts below five per cent of turnover, while keeping the time to process an order below eight business hours. With this goal it becomes much clearer exactly which processes you need to measure.

Once you know the goal and have decided on the measures required to establish it, it is necessary to use benchmarking to check that it's reasonable. Then measure the gap between where you are now (maybe debts are ten per cent of turnover with order processing taking twelve business hours). Finally produce a plan on how to close the gap, by process improvement, maybe by using more resources, maybe even by out-sourcing some of the process.

With these decisions in hand, it is possible to steer towards the goal, by setting performance objectives on team and sub-process owners as sub-goals aimed towards the final goal.

In IT it is, again, often not so simple to decide on appropriate goals. What is important is not to sacrifice customer satisfaction by steering too aggressively towards a difficult goal. This is why the process designs recommended later in this book always include a customer satisfaction process metric to ensure that steering towards important IT goals doesn't end up steering away from customers.

5.5 Accounting

IT Service Management, ITIL in particular, aims to align closely to the goals of the end business customer. These goals are often, if not usually, financial. The ITIL discipline of IT Financial Management deals, as a process, with achieving this. Involving IT Financial Management in the design of metrics early on allows estimates of resource usage to be built into metric design.

For example, it might be established that a service call costs one hundred units. Initially this is probably a very rough estimate, established by dividing the cost of the Service Desk by the number of calls. Over time, this can be refined by providing Financial Management with figures of actual time spent working towards the identified process metrics, KPIs and SLAs and providing notional accounting base on these times.

In the early days this can help identify, for example, SLAs that serve a small part of the business function but absorb large amounts of IT resources. The business may well decide that this is a correct allocation, but, if it is not a business priority then large cost savings can be made.

As the business matures, the cost model will become more sophisticated. At this stage it makes sense to provide metrics for Financial Management to monitor organizational costs overall to spot any trends in the wrong direction and take action to correct the situation before there is a danger of serious cost over-run. It is optimistic to expect this level of sophistication early in the process. Trying to put costing on an accurate basis too early on can be dangerous. The extra pressure is easier for an organization to bear once process based thinking is the norm.

6   Metric Design

Before entering into the detail of particular metrics, it is important to understand the process involved in designing metrics. Otherwise, it is not possible to know if you have a workable set of metrics, however impressive they may appear!

This chapter examines the thought process and methods required to produce a viable set of metrics for an organization.

When discussing metrics for the first time both inside and outside the IT organization, it is important to discuss these principles, so that everybody understands why the process is being followed and what the results will be.

6.1   Basic concepts

Some metrics are easy to measure, your software package is likely to come with lots of metrics 'out of the box'. Some tools have hundreds of them! It would be silly to try to work with metrics that are impossible to measure, but ease of measurement is not a good reason to select a metric!

There are many dangers associated with using metrics that appear easy to measure. The biggest is that they might measure something that you don't want to or need to improve. There is also the danger that a metric that is supplied with your tool looks interesting, but is based on a formula that is subtly different from what you expect.

> For example, a package might offer you 'time to close an incident' as a metric. This might sound like exactly what you want. But, do you know if it measures this time from when somebody calls the Service Desk, from when the call is moved to 'in progress' status or from when it is assigned to somebody? What does the metric measure when the call is 'waiting' for more information from the customer? What does it measure if a call is closed and then re-opened? If the metric reports once a day, what does it do about open calls? Are they counted towards the time calls that are open, or are calls only included in this metric once they have the status 'closed'? How long does it include calls that are closed? Does it include those calls closed in the past day, week, or month?

You have to consider all the above questions when you design a metric, but that means that you have decided on what is best for your organization when you put the metric in place. If you use the metric 'as it comes', you don't know what decisions have been made for you by the designer of the software. They might be what you want, but they might be quite wrong for your organization.

The best solution is to design your own metrics and then see how the metrics provided with your package can be adapted to work exactly as you need them to. This section discusses what you need to think about when you make decisions on exactly what metrics to use.

6.2 Principles

6.2.1 SMART
The acronym SMART (Specific, Measurable, Achievable, Realistic and Timely) has been applied to lots of different business processes. It is a useful set of questions to apply to all metrics before you deploy them.

Does the metric measure a **specific** process or part of a process? If the metric measures parts of two different processes then there is a danger that neither process owner will feel responsible for achieving the result.

Is the metric **measurable**? This is pretty fundamental, but important, you may decide that you need to measure the time your customers are on the 'phone to the Service Desk, but, if you do not have a switchboard or PABX that can give you the times of calls you will not be able to track this.

Is the metric **achievable**? Would it be possible for the Service Desk to close all calls within three minutes? If it takes two minutes to fill in a screen with all the caller's details (if you have a good CMDB this should not be the case, of course!) then you are only allowing one minute to solve the call, which is probably not achievable!

Is the metric **realistic**? Does it make sense to measure the time that incidents keep the status of 'waiting'? There might be lots of different reasons for calls being in this state. If you don't know what the reasons are, then being asked to reduce this time is not realistic, because you would not know where to start. In this case the solution would be to split this status into for example:
• 'Waiting for customer call back'
• 'Waiting for 2nd level Support'
• 'Waiting for software patch'.

The important point is to ask whether this really is measuring something in the real world, rather than something that is just part of the software package.

Is the metric **timely**? If you measure the performance of the Service Desk once a month and one metric is customer satisfaction, based on quarterly surveys, then you don't have a timely metric. Customers could be dissatisfied for two months before your metric would show it!

6.2.2 KISS
Keep It Simple Stupid (KISS) is an unfortunate acronym, but still important. If metrics are not explained well, and how to achieve them not well understood, the door is open to resistance, rejection, disillusionment and easy excuses for non-compliance.

Some people have a very analytical view of the world. This is very useful in IT, where complex problems require a detailed analysis. The danger, with the design of metrics, is that this can lead to complex formulas that measure a few things at the same time. The 'average number of incidents per problem that has an associated change request' could, for example, be a metric. It is possible to understand this, but what does it tell and how could it be improved? Should there be more change requests for problems with lots of incidents or should problems be subdivided so that fewer incidents are associated with them? It just isn't clear why this is important or how it could be improved.

It would be better to step back and ask what is important. Is it the number of incidents per problem? Is it the importance given to problems? Are change requests important in themselves, or are they being used as a measure of the problem solving process? With answers to these questions it might turn out that two or three simple metrics will give a better solution than the first complex one.

6.2.3 GQM Goal - Question - Metrics - Method

Metrics have a long history in Application development. GQM is a method for arriving at metrics that has been used to decide what metrics are required for a software development project.

The method involves designing the top-level goals of the project (in Service Management, these would be the goals of the process). For each goal a set of questions is developed. Each question will be answered if the goal is achieved. Finally, for each goal, a metric to measure the result of the question is developed.

Though this formal method has not been used, the metrics in chapters 7 and 8 have been designed according to such a top down approach. The goal of each process is defined at the top of each section, then the metrics are listed that relate to each goal, while the explanation of the metric essentially answers a question that, if positive, confirms the goal is being met.

6.2.4 MAPE (Mean Absolute Percentage Error)

IT Service Management metrics can produce pure numbers, like so many thousand incidents, so many million network events and so forth. These can be difficult to compare, particularly between organizations or different processes. It is often useful to reduce these to percentages to make them easier to grasp. Various methods are also used to forecast future trends in business.

These can also be used in IT for capacity planning or resource estimation in the future. Will, for example, more people trained to work in the Service Desk be needed next year and, if so, how many? Clearly, measuring workload would be important and we would need to design metrics for this purpose, but we would also need to establish a forecast for next year. We could use all sorts of methods to do this, from a straight forward linear projection to complex simulations. The question will be whether we have a good reliable forecast.

The Mean Absolute Percentage Error is a statistical technique that can help establish if a forecast is reliable. For existing historical data, the measurement of your Service Desk over the past six months, say, and your chosen forecast technique, you can test the reliability by the MAPE formula. If your MAPE is small (much less than 40 per cent) then your forecast is probably reasonably reliable. The formula for calculating this is:

> **MAPE = Σ l(measured values - forecast values) / measured valuesl * 100 / the number of values**

In other words, the sum of the absolute value of the difference between the forecast and the real data divided by the real data as a percentage, divided by the number of values.

6.2.5 Customer Relationship Diagram

Figure 6.1 is an example of a Customer Relationship Diagram. It is a simplification of the complex customer relationships that all processes have. The aim, though, is not to produce a listing of all customer relationships, but to try to identify the most immediate customer of each process.

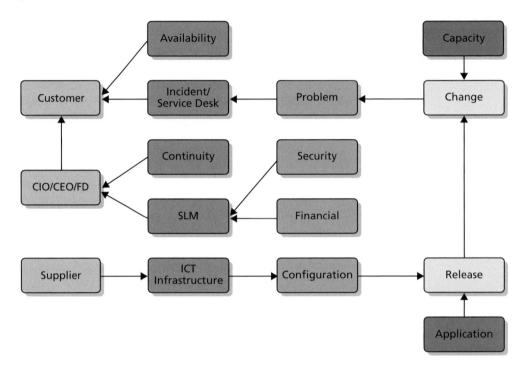

Figure 6.1 Customer Relationship Diagram

The different grayscales represent the steps between the process and the end Customer. Arrows point to the designated primary customer of the process. Additional Stakeholders can be included and alternative primary customers selected depending on local requirements.

The reason for this exercise is to establish where a measurement of customer satisfaction can be made. It is true that there are many stakeholders. Ultimately you could argue that the shareholders give a measure of the overall customer satisfaction of a company by the price that they are prepared to buy shares. This is a very indirect and unsure method of measuring day-to-day satisfaction of an IT process! To simplify the matter down to one single customer ensures a close focus on that customer and also a closer relationship with that customer, to ensure that there are no unpleasant surprises when the satisfaction is measured.

In figure 6.1, the boxes *at the left* show the customers, the *boxes in the second column from the left* the first line processes that get satisfaction measures from the customers themselves. The *boxes in the third column* are second line, measuring their satisfaction from first-line processes. So, for example, Problem Management measures its success by the satisfaction that Incident Management has, how good the Known Error Reports are and how well incidents are reduced by the resolution of underlying problems. Change Management is a third level process, taking its satisfaction measure from Problem Management. In turn, Capacity Management, as a fourth line process, measures customer satisfaction from how satisfied Change Management is with its process operation.

Figure 6.1, again for simplicity, doesn't include other processes that are likely to be involved. A real diagram would include suppliers, sub-contracted parties, and, probably, other business processes or entities that are relevant.

As we will see in later chapters, where the detail of the metrics will be covered, every process has a 'customer satisfaction' metric to satisfy, it is the ultimate guide to the effectiveness of the process, after all! This diagram is a high-level way of understanding how these metrics have been produced.

Before implementing metrics, it is wise to have a workshop with stakeholders and process owners to discuss this diagram and agree that the relationships are correct for the particular situation your organization is in. It might well be, for example, that for a particular organization, it makes more sense for ICT Infrastructure Management to have the Service Desk as its primary customer.

6.3   Requirements

Metrics require properly designed processes to operate effectively. It is possible, and indeed necessary under the Continuous Improvement Process, to change processes over time. But the less often essentials are changed the better. Changing fundamentals of process operation requires careful communication to and possible re-training of everybody involved with the process.

Metrics can only measure from data that is being captured. If problem records, for example, spend time in 'General Root Cause Analysis', 'Fault Tree Analysis' or 'Log File Analysis' phases it will only be possible to measure the relative contribution of these phases if the system is set up to capture these statuses, and if the process actually invokes these statuses appropriately.

It might be unrealistic to expect problem analysts to record their activities in this detail. After all, the objective is to get to the root cause of problems effectively and too much documentation might impede this objective. However, if it is expected that this level will be required then it should be built into the tool customization and process design.

The same applies to categories. Categories of CI, categories of incident, change, problem and so forth. The danger of including a catch-all category of 'General' is well known! It is important to realize, though, that changing categories is a much more frequent activity than changing state transitions.

The prime requirement then is to design processes in such a way that they include the statuses needed to be captured. These statuses must reflect business or process need. Too many statuses, simply for the purpose of completeness or possible measurement, are also counterproductive.

This means that metric design must occur early on in the overall ITIL implementation for best effect. If metrics are to be retrofitted after processes have already been implemented this needs to be very carefully designed, managed and implemented through the Release Management process - to make sure that the implications are properly communicated to all who are affected and that the documentation is properly managed under change control.

People are only human. If it appears that the correct use of status codes or categories is not important then important data will be lost as insufficient care is taken in recording the appropriate changes. Thus, it's important to monitor and manage the proper use of these, and to add preventive controls, making sure things are being done correctly. For example, if it is not logical to change from status P2 to P7 the application shouldn't let us do it. This includes communicating information gleaned from analysis of process data, contributions to process improvement and breakthroughs in Problem Management, as a result of proper data recording.

To summarize this:
- Design processes in such a way that the appropriate statuses are in place from the start.
- If changes to the process flow are made, ensure communication and training is thorough.
- Do not include any catch-all statuses or categories.
- Monitor and manage the proper use of statuses and categories.

6.4   Design individual metrics

Designing metrics is not a technical or back-office job. For metrics to work, all parties must be consulted. Customers, and important stakeholders must be satisfied that the metrics are an accurate measure of what is happening in the processes and that they can rely on them for their information. Process owners must, in turn, be satisfied that they can be held accountable to succeed in achieving the required measures and have some hope of exceeding them through concerted effort.

To arrive at this situation, a set of possible metrics can be proposed to a workshop where process owners and stakeholders are present. Then each metric and its implications is discussed in turn. Modifications can be made and metrics can be replaced with more appropriate ones. In the end all parties realize that they might be altered in future, but that there is a consensus to use the set agreed.

This is a fundamentally important step. After this has been done, until the metrics are revised, the process owners have agreed to be accountable. And the stakeholders in the process have agreed to accept the results of the metrics as a fair reflection of how well things have been going. This means that future discussions can be based on an agreed set of standards. Thus, they can focus on the issues raised by metrics not met and how to resolve them, rather than wasting time discussing how appropriate they might be.

The very first time round, during benchmarking, the IT manager or service manager may decide on a set of metrics without this consultation. This is a reasonable step to beta-test the processes, establish some preliminary benchmark data and check that the metrics can be produced in a timely manner. Ironing out these matters is wise, but, once the beta test is over, it is vital to consult the stakeholders and agree on a set of metrics to measure and control the live operation.

6.5   Design integrated sets of metrics

It is possible to design metrics for the different ITIL processes in isolation from each other. This is ultimately unsatisfactory as it doesn't allow management to compare how well the different areas are working as processes.

Friendly competition between process owners to have the best operation is a healthy contributor to high quality processes. If the metrics between different organizations are too different then this is not possible. One can't compare apples with oranges.

In order to have comparable metrics, it is best to have the same number of metrics, as far as possible and without missing the focus on what is really important for the process. The metrics should be presented and ordered in priority as equally as possible.

This also allows IT administration to merge the metrics from the different processes and produce a top-level management report showing how the organization is performing as a process enabled operation.

The focus on the most important customer for each process enables the customer satisfaction metric to be measured weekly or monthly, so that fair comparison can be made.

Finally, designing metrics for different processes so that they have the same 'look and feel', even though they are measuring different things, helps process owners feel that they are being treated fairly. The different processes put different strains on people. Incident Management is stressful and requires high energy, whilst Contingency Management requires careful and meticulous planning. Despite these differences, integrated metrics can unify process managers as a team, understanding the different tempo of work, but recognizing when it has been done particularly well.

Celebration of success in an organization is vital to morale, helps individual growth and inspires a culture of excellence. If rewards are felt to be unfairly made, this undermines this positive environment. Integrated sets of metrics enable rewards to the best performers to be made with no possibility of suspicion of favouritism or unfairness. So this is an important step for overall morale, not something to be underestimated in importance!

6.6   Examples of bad and good metrics

We must all have, at some time, been told by a Service Desk person that he must 'close the call' and, if we have the incident again 'open a new call'. We have probably wondered why we should know anything about the internal workings of the organization and been bemused at why the person speaking to us finds it more important to open or close calls than to deal with our question or incident.

This is an example of poor, unhelpful or uninformative metric setting. People in these call centres are being measured on how quickly they close calls. This means that they have an incentive to close them as quickly as possible, even if the person calling is not yet satisfied. They soon learn that opening a new call keeps their closing average (metric) low, so they are seen by management to be performing well.

The cost, of course, is poor customer satisfaction as we end up feeling that we are just objects, calls to be dealt with, rather than customers needing help. This is not what a business needs!

6.6.1 How can this be rectified?

One easy way is to include customer satisfaction as a measure. If the customer is satisfied, even if a call has been closed and a new one opened unnecessarily, then all should be well. This is the 'metric balancing' method.

Another way is to add another metric that measures how many calls the same customer makes in a week on the same subject. This should catch out the operators who have been closing calls just to make the stats good.

Sadly, neither of these methods works very well. The first is a good start, customer satisfaction is important. However, we all know what will happen. The call will be closed and a new one opened, but the person will say 'management insist on this', so as to get a good report from you the customer, while leaving you unhappy with the anonymous 'management' instead. Not a great improvement for the Company!

The second 'solution' is even more dangerous. Firstly, if this is the standard solution you end up with your staff thinking that you are just setting metrics to 'catch them out' (and you are). Secondly, there is a solution for the Service Desk person: simply open new calls with a different subject. This means that the new metric will not catch them out. However, it means that your business statistics no longer makes sense. You really don't want to give the Service Desk an incentive to use the wrong category or subject because incident solving and market research will end up misled, with possibly very expensive results!

6.6.2 So, how can we square this circle?

Using the methods outlined in this chapter, the first question that would come to mind is: has the process owner agreed to this measure of the 'time to close calls'? Probably not. Why is it so important to close calls quickly anyway? You can see some answers to this, it keeps the customer happy to have his incidents solved (if it is solved, if a new call is opened this objective is not being met). It means that the centre can process more calls for the same number of people, but, of course, this isn't true if lots of the calls are simply reopened calls for the same incident!

The next question is: 'have the stakeholders (the people calling) been consulted?' Do they want the calls to be as short as possible? Probably not, they probably would rather not know about calls being 'opened' or 'closed', but want to know if their call is solved.

6.6.3 So, is there a better metric?

Well, yes, there must be! But let us think of the process of setting metrics first. Shouldn't we go back to the drawing board, consult our stakeholders and process owners and work out what the real objectives are? Then use them to propose better metrics.

This isn't a crossword puzzle or other game where points are scored for the cleverest metric design. It is a matter of improving the process so that it delivers more to the end customers.

For a start, might it not be better to have all calls that last over a certain time passed to a Problem Management team to find out why they took so long? Then, if particular issues can be discovered and workarounds provided call times will reduce of themselves.

The problem is simply not thinking of where the priority lies, with the customer, but assuming that the metric is a matter of controlling the staff in the Service Desk (or call centre). If Service Desk staff feel that they have support in improving the service they deliver then they will work harder and better. Their morale will be higher too as they have some elements of influence in the process as they describe why some calls take longer than others. A vital part of contentment is having some control over your environment, so this helps with that as well. The virtuous circle continues as the more contented staff communicate this through more relaxed calls with customers that don't include requests to 'close' or 're-open' calls!

7 Practical Metric Production

This chapter uses one set of metrics to explain the thought process and method behind the choice of metrics. The following chapter 'Specific Metrics for IT Service Management' introduces a set of metrics for all the Service Management processes.

This chapter is a link between the theory in the first six chapters and the actual metrics shown as examples. This link is necessary to explain how the choice of metrics conforms to the recommendations made - and where it deviates from them. This will help in deciding whether to implement the metrics as-is or to modify them.

For the purpose of using the metrics as management and steering information, a metric chart is used. This chapter also explains how these metric charts work and what the different fields are. It uses the Configuration Management process to explain the principles of metric production, as this process is fundamental to Service Management, being one of the central control processes identified by ISO20000.

Though the process usually used as an example is Incident Management, because it is easy for people to think up various metrics that may or may not be useful, choosing the easiest process as an example is unhelpful and potentially misleading. This makes Configuration Management a better candidate than processes with fewer dependencies.

7.1 Reasons for metric choices: Configuration Management as an example

Besides Customer Satisfaction, we chose seven Configuration Management metrics for the reasons given in the preceding chapters - to be simple, easy to understand (Keep It Simple Stupid, KISS), specific, measurable, achievable, realistic and timely (SMART) as described. They have also been chosen to match the objective, aim or target of the process in question. For this reason this is quoted at the start of each process in the appendices.

> **Relating metrics to process objectives is a crucial step in the development of metrics: it will distinguish the *meaningful metrics* from the *measurable metrics*.**

According to OGC's ITIL Best Practice for Service Support, in the case of Configuration Management, the process goals are:
1. Account for all the IT assets and configurations within the organization and its services.
2. Provide accurate information on configurations and their documentation to support all the other Service Management processes, like Incident, Problem, Change and Release Management.
3. Verify the configuration records against the infrastructure and correct any exceptions.

From these process goals, we can derive one single metric objective, using the principles discussed in chapter one to six. Summarizing the three main goals would provide us with such a metric objective. From the Configuration Management process goals, we could derive the following specific **metric objective:** "to identify and manage the IT infrastructure information and relationships accurately and effectively according to business need and agreed policy standards". In this specification, identifying the IT infrastructure information represents the steps of verifying and providing accurate information, and managing the IT infrastructure information can be seen as accounting for it.

Every metric should follow directly from this metric objective, in order to support the measurability of the metrics, to simplify them, to find more specific metrics, et cetera. Only then we will eventually measure meaningful values, and not just measurable values.

As the processes mature and develop, the level of interconnection between process blocks will begin to increase. As the maturity level approaches optimization, the metric level and count start to decrease, as the real control metrics are more clearly understood, compound metrics become more dominate and the need for numerous lower-level metrics starts to decline as they start to appear as 'noise'. This long term trend will result in different sets of metrics in different organizations over time, optimized to their own particular requirements.

In the appendices we'll introduce metric objectives for a lot of IT Service Management processes. We now consider each metric in turn for the example process of Configuration Management.

7.1.1 Customer Satisfaction

The early introduction of the Customer Relationship Diagram in this book made clear that Customer Satisfaction was going to be a vital focus. Each process is matched with its 'main', 'closest', 'most important' or 'key' customer - even though all members of the organization are ultimately working towards satisfying the end customer, a more immediate and relevant yardstick for each process is the interfacing process, or processes.

All measures of Customer Satisfaction are based on either a Customer Survey, or a particular Customer Satisfaction rating given for a completed piece of work - an outcome of a process. The recommendation is that each process establishes a point where the output to the 'key' customer can be said to be complete or closed sufficiently for the customer to provide a contemporaneous satisfaction score.

As used here the 'Customer Satisfaction' metric applies to customer reports after they have called in with Service Calls, and to surveys sent out to canvas customers for their level of satisfaction. The score given here is arbitrary and a different method might give a different percentage or other value. What is important is that this is measured and that this measure is shown to be important to management.

For certain processes, the closeness to the customer makes this even more important. In these cases, the organization wide customer satisfaction score can be replaced with a score for this particular process or organization. If a survey is sent out that has questions relating to different processes or organizations, then the results can be apportioned to the relevant metric rather than simply having one metric for the entire organization.

Customer Surveys are very important. In particular, being general, they enable the business to target customers who might not have contacted the Service Desk or been involved with many of the other processes for which satisfaction scores are required. Unfortunately, these surveys are expensive and take time. In particular they take the time of the customer being surveyed and, if done too frequently, they can be irritating and cause in themselves of dissatisfaction.

For these reasons Customer Surveys cannot satisfy the need for timely measurement of the effectiveness of Service Management processes. The metrics in this book rely upon more timely feedback covering work just done. The closing of an incident, problem, or release, for example, is an opportunity for the customer to comment on the level of satisfaction as well as to make recommendations for improvement.

In some processes, it is difficult to identify appropriate measurement points. In this case, some more or less artificial, but timely feedback mechanism that overcomes the problems of a Customer Survey might need to be devised. A weekly meeting to discuss satisfaction with the manager of the 'key' process might be an appropriate mechanism - in effect a stripped down and frequent Customer Survey.

In our Metric Chart, Customer Satisfaction is given as a number between 0 and 5, where 0 indicates completely unsatisfied and 5 meaning completely satisfied. The target value is 4 and the danger level <3.

In respect to Configuration Management it is worth while pointing out, that the Customer Relationship Diagram (Figure 6.1) shows Release Management as the process chosen as the 'main' customer for Configuration Management. The objectives of Configuration Management explicitly mention Incident, Problem, Change and Release Management, so any one of these could also have been a justifiable choice in the diagram. Release Management is, however, responsible for large changes to the infrastructure, so it is important that these are properly reflected in the CMDB and this gives a reason why it is a particularly important process for Configuration Management.

It is also worth noting, from Figure 7.1, that, though this metric is from one process, it is made up of three sub-processes, ensuring that we measure not just the end result when a particular release is closed, but also important milestones during the planning and implementation of the release. Where possible it would be ideal if other Customer Satisfaction metrics could also be made up of distinct checkpoints where the process contributes. Things are not always this clear-cut though.

It can be argued that the merging of three metrics could mean that an error in the CMDB could lead to three, apparently separate, poor Customer Satisfaction ratings for the same error. This might be felt not to be fair to the process owner. Though it is true that the error could give three bad ratings, this need not be the case. If the first error causes a Planning Error, then there is time, after that has been highlighted and the poor score received, to correct the CMDB. This avoids the other two bad scores - in fact, doing a particularly efficient job in making the corrections, and making sure that a process change request is made to prevent re-occurrence (if this makes sense) might give a very good score in the final Release Review.

7.1.2 Number of Licenses not used

At first glance this appears to be a much more specific metric than most others - that is because it is! Software licenses are a major cost to organizations. It is the responsibility of Configuration Management to keep track of, and help in making sure that the correct number of licenses are owned, deployed and paid for. This task has a very visible and direct influence on the financial effectiveness of IT as seen by the Business. Making this task in Configuration Management the specific object of a metric is unusual - in most other processes, we would not select something so specific.

This is justified in this case because the measure is simple (KISS), directly associated with a Configuration Management task as defined in ITIL and ISO20000 and, at the same time, a useful audit point for the general level of accuracy in the CMDB. In order to be sure of the correct number of licenses, it is necessary to be sure that all CIs are in the CMDB and that the linkage between license and CI and user is correct - having these relationships properly set up goes to the heart of good Configuration Management.

This same measure could be described in different ways. It would be possible to count the percentage of licenses actually used in the last month or the number of licenses for which the software has not been used for six months as an indication of licenses that could, possibly, be dispensed with. There is nothing wrong with these alternatives, and they might be preferred, but they are less straightforward than this one and it is not quite so easy to see how much money would be saved by reducing the metric.

Another value of this metric is the effort needed to actually measure it. If software tools are to be bought, they will need to be able to report on not only licenses that have been bought and owned (as CIs), but also on the relationships between them and those using them. A 10-user license for X software product can be reported properly as being used by 6 users, for example, and so that the next user to deploy product X gets the next one of these licenses. This is instead of having another 10-user license ordered! If the software tool used supports the production of the correct figures for this metric, then it is likely to be able to contribute in reducing the cost of software licenses and keeping CMDB relationships up-to-date in real time.

Quite a few benefits from one, rather unusual, metric!

7.1.3 Number of failed RFCs from bad CMDB data

Change and Configuration Management are the very closely linked 'Control Processes' in ISO20000. RFCs act on Configuration Items. If the information is wrong, possibly the software release, or the owner, or even a missing CI, the RFC can fail and be referred back to the originator for re-submission. If this is because the CMDB is faulty, the RFC will be counted under this metric.

This is a measure not just of how well the CMDB is maintained, but also of how errors in the CMDB are affecting another crucial process.

Change Management is identified as one of the key customers of Configuration Management; it is a very closely linked process and Configuration Management relies upon its good operation for the maintenance of the CMDB.

This metric makes it clear that maintaining the CMDB is not simply and end in itself, but an important part of the overall functioning of Service Management. It provides an important balance to metric 7.1.7 - the number of RFCs without corresponding CI updating - it is not good enough to have 95 per cent of the items in the CMDB accurate if there are still RFCs failing because of bad CI information!

7.1.4 Number of unauthorized configurations

Many processes rely upon a known set of configurations being implemented in the environment. The range of attributes possible for particular baseline (sometimes 'benchmark') CIs are known and restricted in number.

The audit will discover configurations that do not conform to the authorized set, but that often is an annual or semi-annual process.

Unauthorized configurations may appear to those that implement them to be as effective as those that are authorized. However, they can impact on hardware and software repair and recovery times.

For example, a standard router configuration may call for a particular manufacturer X, model Y if, say a 32 port router of given capacity is to be used. Manufacturer Z may have a faster model and, if purchasing is not properly controlled, this might be ordered and implemented in part of the infrastructure. Since the organization does not have spare components or swappable units in the Definite Hardware Store, a failure in this component might lead to a long downtime and failure of SLA. The discovery of such an unauthorized configuration - or, ideally, its avoidance through control of purchasing - can prevent this problem.

After a merger with another company, this may well be a very large number as the equipment used by the two companies might have been very different. This metric can then be used to reflect how well Configuration Management is operating to either replace incompatible configurations or to include new configurations in the relevant processes so that they can be authorized.

This metric also drives the decision on what tools are to be used in managing the environment. Automated checking of CIs that show properly authorized configurations against equipment, or software actually installed can turn up discrepancies that will originally contribute to this metric, but through structured Release Management, can be reduced to acceptable levels.

7.1.5 Number of incidents from failed changes caused by wrongly documented CIs

Changes are reflected in the CMDB. If the wrong CI has been updated, deleted or added this may later cause an incident. If the CMDB is not correct then it may cause the wrong CI to be affected in the environment with the same result.

When an incident is closed showing the cause is related to a change then there is a very high probability that there is an involvement with Configuration Management - but this obviously needs to be established for certain to make it a useful metric for Configuration Management.

This metric puts focus on the importance of clean, accurate Configuration Management data to the Change Management process as well as making sure that the two 'Control Process' owners identified by ISO20000 keep very close communication.

7.1.6 Number of breached SLA because of CMDB errors

There is a danger that process metrics can be too internally focused. This ensures that, despite Configuration Management not being a customer facing process, its contribution to service levels is still a priority for the process owner.

SLA breaches will be subject to investigation by Service Level Management, with Problem Management investigating the underlying causes. If any feature of the CMDB (missing items, misleading relationships, poor escalation because of CIs not being properly linked to the appropriate SLA being just some examples) has contributed directly to a breached SLA, it will appear in this metric. Any examples will be an urgent focus for the Configuration Management process owner.

Though this metric will probably be zero in most instances, its presence highlights the importance of SLAs to internal processes. With a mature CMDB, SLA failures will not often be caused by CMDB errors. However, we are, in this book, considering organizations that are not necessarily at a high level of maturity (otherwise they'd have all their metrics in place). So we must consider things that are likely during the early stages of CMDB implementation. During these stages, incidents and problems will be shown to be caused by CMDB errors and some of these will impact SLAs. As the organization matures, though, this metric can, and should, be phased out through the SIP.

The process owner is likely to pay some attention to escalated incidents to make sure that there is no CMDB contribution to the incident - this attention may be sufficient to bring the proper resources to bear on an incident to resolve it before there is a breach.

7.1.7 Number of RFCs without corresponding CI updating

For every RFC, the CMDB has to be updated at a point specified in the policies and process. This metric gives the extent to which control procedures are adhered to. This in turn affects the accuracy of the CMDB and impacts any subsequent changes and releases by not providing correct information on the CIs.

This can usually be measured easily by reports from the tool used by ICT Operations to monitor events - at least if these components can be detected automatically. Items discovered by this tool that are not in the CMDB are, by definition, not authorized. This can be caused by an illegal change, by an improper change where the CMDB was not updated, or - and this is the least serious cause - by a properly handled ongoing change where the CMDB has not yet been updated according to plan. It is obvious that the first two causes should be considered here. The size of the discrepancy can highlight security issues or areas where Release or Change Management are not being effective.

7.1.8 Percentage of inaccurate CIs

Inaccurate CIs can be detected by the errors they cause in other processes - this will be picked up by a number of the metrics above. It is important that the Configuration Management process is also active in improving the quality of the CMDB without simply reacting to errors that are discovered. Though annual, six-monthly, or even more frequent physical audits will give a good measure of how bad the situation is, it is important that checks are regularly made and that this metric ensures that proper attention is focused on this activity.

Actually measuring this can be a challenge. It is important that a metric is SMART - which includes the 'M' of Measurable. The operation tool used for ICT event management usually has a database containing, at least, physical CIs, that can be used to verify the content of the CMDB at least weekly. In addition, the Service Desk can check, at every call, that the details for a particular caller are correct - any mismatches can be referred to Configuration Management and included as part of this measurement.

It will be important to agree exactly what measurements will contribute to this metric - and this will depend on the toolset used. This is quoted as a percentage, rather than a raw number, because it reflects how well the Configuration Process is actually working.

7.2   Data Model for Measuring Metrics

Every process consists of a number of sub-processes. These can be used to return a value when there is a state change and this value can be used as a metric.

All processes have a Customer Satisfaction metric, so we will consider the data model using that metric. Many processes are 'internal' processes of the IT services organization: there is no direct interaction with the users of the IT services. In these cases the 'customers' are internal as well (management, other processes). Please note that there will always be one or more stakeholders for a process. As has been noted, one of the key customers of Configuration Management is Release Management. Therefore, we use this process to determine the Customer Satisfaction about Configuration Management in this section.

When a metric is designed, a diagram similar to figure 7.1 can be produced. This shows the sub-states that return values that will make up the metric. This usually works in two possible ways. Either the process returns a value, which is used, as is the case here, or a count, or tally, of the state transitions is kept. For example if we were counting the number of releases, this could be produced by counting each 'Complete Release Review' state instead of getting a customer satisfaction value back from it.

The scope of the Customer Satisfaction metric for Configuration Management therefore grasps the whole process, from the start until the end. This is indicated by the two arrows from the start and the end, pointing towards the Customer Satisfaction measurement.

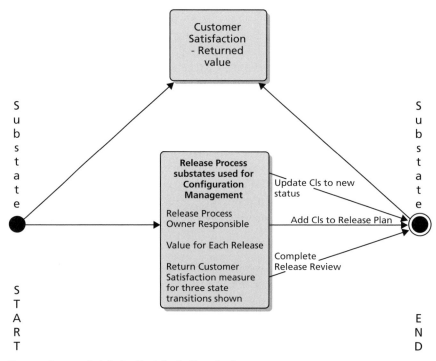

Figure 7.1 Customer Satisfaction Metric for Configuration Process

Figure 7.1 shows three sub-states that form part of the Release Management process:
- Update CIs to new status
- Add CIs to Release Plan
- Complete Release Review

As CIs are used to document a release, a particular CI has a status of 'due for release' before it is updated and 'updates with release' afterwards. The effectiveness of this process, and the reporting of the status of a release during its implementation is what is used to judge the quality of Configuration Management.

These three sub-processes are the parts of the overall Release Management process that concern us here as they are the places where Configuration Items (an output of the Configuration Management process) are used. This is where the Release Management process owner (or the person delegated to the task) is able to consider how well the Configuration Management process has contributed to the task in hand. This is a subjective view, as all Customer Satisfaction measures are.

The process owner will form it after considering how accurate and up to date the CI information was and how easy it was to find the affected CIs for the particular release. In addition, how easy it was to include their 'desired state' into the Release Plan and then to move them to the new status when the release was complete. Finally, the process owner will be able to return a value that summarizes how the Configuration Management process contributed to the overall release during the Release Review.

This method means that each release will contribute three Customer Satisfaction measures to Configuration Management. One comes from the planning stage, one from the implementation stage and one at the review stage of the stakeholder "Release Management". This gives a well-rounded view of the contribution whilst not involving the Release Management process in giving opinions on the process too often.

7.3 Prioritizing and scoring the metrics

In order to report one metric value for each process during each period, it is necessary to have a method of combining the metric values. There are many ways of doing this. The example method outlined here, is to give a priority to each of the eight metrics, from 1-8, with 1 for the least important metric and 8 for the most. These values are then used as the weights. Some metrics are percentages, others can take on virtually any value, and so it is not possible to use them directly.

Using the **Target**, however, it is possible to judge success or failure for a metric. The scoring system used here gives three values (as in the Balanced Scorecard Traffic Light system). Red for a score well off Target, beyond the Danger value used as a threshold here, in fact. Amber for a value between the Danger value and the Target value. Green for on Target or above.

Once we have these as well, it is simply a matter of giving high weight to success in a high priority metric so forth, summing the results to give an overall score.

The management benefit of this is that it is possible to change the priority of the metrics over time to reflect the changing needs of the business or the maturity of the processes. In the early days of the Configuration Management process, it might be optimistic to expect large reductions in incidents by supporting other processes with an excellent CMDB.

For this reason it would be reasonable to have this objective to have a relaxed Target and Danger setting (one that can be achieved reasonably easily) and a low priority. Once Configuration Management has matured to the level where the percentage of inaccurate CIs reported is always small (probably a very high priority in the early days), it can be demoted to a lower priority whilst the reduction of incidents can be raised in priority to present an improvement challenge to the process owner.

Setting targets is a management responsibility that requires judgement as well as analytical ability. The benchmark (or baseline) measure of a particular process might be close to the optimum or it might be a very long way from it. A manager must have an understanding of the people and technology that underly the process, as well as the process maturity so as to be able to set targets that show the proper level of ambition whilst still being achievable. Simply adding five per cent to a baseline, for example, is not going to be effective as this might be easy for some processes but impossible for others. In the early days, when processes are immature, some rule of thumb like five per cent can be used, but it is important for management to work to understand enough about all the processes so that more effective, tailored targets can be established as processes mature.

There are many ways of calculating the score. The simplest is the following:

$$\text{Total Score} = \sum_{N=1}^{8} PN*RN$$

Where PN is the priority of the Nth metric. RN is the result during this period, being 1 for Green, 0 for amber, -1 for Red.

Metric	Danger	Target	Actual	Priority/ Weight	Resu
1 Customer Satisfaction	<3	4	2	3	-1
2 Number of licenses not used	>10	5	3	2	1
3 Number of failed RFCs from bad CMDB data	>20	10	15	7	0
4 Number of unauthorized configurations	>15	5	2	8	1
5 Number of incidents from failed changes caused by wrongly documented CIs.	>6	0	0	6	1
6 Number of breached SLA because of CMDB errors	>2	0	0	1	1
7 Number of RFCs without corresponding CI updating	<90	95	20	4	1
8 Percentage of inaccurate CIs	>100	40	10	5	1

Table 7.1 Metric results

Given the results in table 7.1, the calculation is:

Total Score = 3*-1 + 2*1 + 7*0 + 8*1 + 6*1 + 1*1 + 4*1 + 5*1 =
-3 + 2 + 0 + 8 + 6 +1 + 4 + 5 = 23

This is out of a maximum of 36 and a minimum of -36: if all values would have been green (+1), the sum would have been (1 + 2 + 3 + 4 + 5 + 6 + 7 + 8) * 1 = 36 and when all would have been red (-1), this would have been -36.

If you should want to make the resulting value independent of the number of metrics per process, you could simply divide all values by the number of metrics, to obtain a comparable result. This would produce the value 23/8 = 2.9 out of a maximum of 4.5. In another scenario you could choose to work with percentages by dividing the obtained sum by the maximum value; this would produce the value 0.64 (or 64 per cent). Both values would make process outcomes comparable to each other. An example of a company result table could then look like this:

Process	Total score	Previous score	Result
Configuration Management	+0.71	+0.68	+0.03
Change Management	+0.84	+0.88	-0.04
Service Level Management	+0.55	+0.47	+0.08
Financial Management	-0.24	-0.34	+0.10

Table 7.2 Scoring metrics

This approach could feed the maturity level of each process, and as a result of the IT services organization.

As illustrated above, organizations can choose from several methods of quantifying their results. Most important is to have a clear philosophy of how to use these methods, and how to interpret the results, before starting with any measurement programme.

Table 7.3 is the quantative metric chart in the format that can be used in a management information system. The metrics have also been numbered for reference purposes here.

Metric	Danger	Target	Possible Values
1 Customer Satisfaction	<3	4	0 - 5
2 Number of licenses not used	>10	5	Unlimited
3 Number of failed RFCs from bad CMDB data	>20	10	Unlimited
4 Number of unauthorized configurations	>15	5	Unlimited
5 Number of incidents from failed changes aused by wrongly documented CIs.	>6	0	Unlimited
6 Number of breached SLAs because of CMDB errors	>2	0	Unlimited
7 Number of RFCs without corresponding CI updating	<90	95	Unlimited
8 Percentage of inaccurate CIs	>100	40	0-100

Table 7.3 The metric chart for Configuration Management

In the appendices, we'll suggest lots of metrics in a fixed dataform. This way, you could easily use these metrics in a Metric Chart shown in table 7.3. Suggestions on using this chart will be given in chapter 10.4.1: The presentation of metrics.

8 Specific Metrics for IT Service Management

After explaining the method used to construct the metrics introduced in this book, we now provide examples of metrics that can be used for **Service Management processes**. They include, as a subset, the ITIL process areas. But they also add Programme and Project Management as well as Functional User Support. Rather than the familiar ITIL division into 'Service Support' and 'Service Delivery', the processes are divided into 'Operational', 'Tactical' and 'Strategic', depending on their type of goals: short term (operational), medium term (tactical) or long term (strategical). There's a separate section for Programme and Project Management metrics.

The metrics for Operational Service Management Processes will deal with:
• Incident Management
• Service Desk
• Configuration Management
• Change Management
• Release Management (including Application Management)
• Operations Management (including Infrastructure Management)

The metrics for Tactical Service Management Processes will deal with:
• Service Level Management
• Problem Management
• Financial Management for IT services
• Capacity Management
• IT Service Continuity Management
• Availability Management
• Security Management

The metrics for Strategic Service Management Processes will deal with:
• Business Perspective Metrics
• Continuous Service Improvement Programme (SIP)
• Risk Management
• Documentation Management
• Competence, Awareness and Training (CAT)

And finally there'll be a separate sub chapter on Programme and Project Management.

For detailed descriptions on these metrics, please check the appendices. In that section, they are all specified, explained, and justified. The appendix number for each process is mentioned in parentheses.

In the appendices, for each process the **Process Goals** are described, a **Mission Statement** is provided, and the most likely **process owner** is indicated. Then the specific **Objectives** of the process are described.

Per objective one or more **metrics** are provided. Each metric is related to one specific **metric objective** - which objective of a process is measured with this metric; all metrics will be grouped per objective.

The metrics shown are examples and can be modified to suit any particular organizational model or set of requirements, using the principles outlined in the first eight chapters. They can also, however, be adopted as-is. The examples are presented as they could be implemented in a spreadsheet. Many organizations will find it more useful to automate the collection, graphing and distribution of metrics using custom software, databases and webservers. But this mechanism does not alter the nature of the metrics themselves, so the spreadsheet method is used throughout this book.

The sheets used to describe the specific metrics for IT Service Management have the following fields:
- **Metric** - this field describes the metric as simply as possible. The Units used in the metric are appended in braces {}.
- **Description** - a short line to describe the metric, in addition the wording in the title.
- **Specification** - a short line to specify exactly what is measured and/or how this is done.
- **Justification** - an explanation why this metric is useful and meaningful.
- **Audience** - an indication of whom the metric is supposed to provide with useful information.
- **Constraints** - any issues that limit the application or interpretation of the metric.
- **Danger value** - the condition for the state of this metric to be red.
- **Target** - the target value for this metric.
- **Possible Values** - the list of values that this metric can hold.

The last three fields are the quantitative fields, enabling the metrics to be used in a management information system. All values in the following paragraphs are examples of an imaginary organization, and should be customized to your local situation. Where these thresholds should be set in your organization, depends on the results of benchmarking, the level of tolerance that the process owner requires, and the ambition level of the process objectives. Simply for consistency, all values here have been given a Danger and Target value.

The **Danger** field indicates where the threshold is set to alert the process owner that the metric indicates an underlying problem that needs investigation. This is set originally after benchmarking has indicated an appropriate figure - the figures given in this book are for illustration purposes, so that the example graphs in chapter 10.4.1 can be related back to the metrics. In the case of the first metric, 'Customer Satisfaction', the intention is to trigger a threshold when a level of satisfaction less than 3 is returned. This is signalling that things are a lot worse than the Target value. If this arrangement is found confusing, it is perfectly reasonable to set Danger to the Target value and have only one threshold.

The **Target** is the level that the process owner has agreed, with those responsible for implementing the process, to aim for. As mentioned above, this level would be agreed after benchmarking had indicated what levels were obtainable (before a PIR). Benchmarking values can be derived from market standards (based on values from other, comparable, companies) or from values achieved in the past. Based on the expected capacity to improve, a specific Target value can be set.

It would also be possible to have a **Warning** field, set at, say, 3.5 to indicate that the level was close to the Target level and trigger on that.

Possible Values lists the range that the metric could take. For a percentage it is usually listed as from 0-100, though some percentage values might show more than hundred per cent and this range should show that if it is possible. 'Unlimited' indicates that the field returns a number with out any obvious constraint.

Values can be **numbers** or **percentages**. In many cases a number could be changed into a percentage, by comparing it to a total. Which of these value types would be most significant and meaningful depends upon context factors.

In all cases a value must be measured over a specific period of time, to comply to the "T" in SMART, e.g. per day, per week, per month. A percentage can be a hard percentage or a sliding average. Most values will change over time.

Danger Values are always higher or lower than Target Values. Depending on the local situation, the relative maturity of the organization, and the point in time, the Danger Value can be set relatively higher or lower.

It is important to implement some process measures. Otherwise it is not possible to know if things are improving. A continuous Service Improvement Programme as explained in section 8.3.2 will allow metrics to evolve to suit the organization more closely over time. One major advantage of adopting the processes 'as is' is that it is then possible to compare experiences and even benchmark data with other organizations that have chosen the same route.

ISO20000 or your country equivalent's (e.g. SANS15000 in South Africa and AS8018 in Australia), as well as COBIT and Six Sigma all advocate the use of metrics, so quick progress in implementing Service Management process metrics can help in progress towards meeting goals in these areas as well.

8.1   Metrics for Operational Service Management Processes

8.1.1 Incident Management (A)
Metrics for Incident Management are:
- Percentage of incidents resolved by 1st Line Support
- Average call time with no escalation
- Percentage of incidents incorrectly assigned
- Percentage of incidents resolved within target time by priority

- Average time for second level support to respond
- Average time to resolve incidents
- Percentage of incidents re-assigned
- Percentage of incidents incorrectly categorized
- Percentage of time 1st line support bypassed
- Customer Satisfaction
- Percentage of calls that are service requests
- Percentage of incidents solved rightly the first time (First Time Right Resolution)
- Percentage of proactively solved incidents

8.1.2 Service Desk (B)

Service Desk metrics are:
- Number of calls per agent
- Percentage of calls closed first time per agent
- Number of calls that exceed SLA
- Number of calls escalated to second Level Support
- Customer Satisfaction
- Number of calls escalated to third Level Support
- Average time waiting for call to be answered
- Average time spent trying to contact customers per call
- Percentage of calls that come via the web
- Percentage of calls with wrong escalation
- Percentage of calls dropped by users
- Percentage of calls converted to tickets
- Percentage of incidents from event management
- Percentage of calls rightly assigned the first time (First time right assignment)

8.1.3 Configuration Management (C)

Metrics for Configuration Management are:
- Number of licenses not used
- Number of failed RFCs from bad CMDB data
- Number of unauthorized configurations
- Number of incidents from failed changes caused by wrongly documented CIs
- Number of breached SLA because of CMDB errors
- Number of RFCs without corresponding CI updating
- Percentage of inaccurate CIs
- Customer Satisfaction

8.1.4 Change Management (D)

Metrics for Change Management are:
- Percentage of failed changes
- Percentage of rejected RFCs
- Number of unauthorized changes
- Change backlog
- Outages during changes
- Number of failed changes with no back-out plan

- Percentage of changes on time
- Percentage of changes causing incidents
- Number of CAB items not actioned on time
- Customer Satisfaction
- Number of Emergency Changes
- Number of changes that do not deliver the expected results

8.1.5 Release Management (E)

Please note that Release Management includes the activities described in the ITIL publication on Application Management: application releases are the bulk of the releases we'll see in practice, but in the end these are still releases - and therefore they will be handled within the Release Management process as described in the ITIL core books.

In this chapter we'll first deal with general, more high-level Release Management issues, and then go into details on aspects of Application Support and Application Development.

Metrics for Release Management are:
- Installed software packages not in DSL
- Number of urgent releases
- Number of incidents caused by release
- Percentage of releases on time
- Number of untested releases
- Average cost of release
- Number of unused software licenses
- Percentage of accuracy of release estimates
- Customer satisfaction

Application Support (E.1)

Application Support metrics are:
- Number of bugs investigated
- Number of optimizations
- Number of applications/revisions released to production
- Number of end-user training sessions
- Number of defects detected from log files
- Number of fixes tested and released to production
- Number of fixes returned to development

Application Development (E.2)

Application Development metrics are:
- Number of defects found during development or testing
- Number of defects fixed during testing
- Number of reported bugs fixed
- Number of applications/revisions accepted as deployed
- Number of applications/revisions rejected by Application Support
- Number of application designs signed off by business
- Number of successful application builds
- Number of days deployment slipped

8.1.6 Operations Management/ICT Infrastructure Management (F)

Operations Management is seen by the ITIL as a subset of ICT Infrastructure Management, which consists of the processes 'Design and Planning', 'Deployment', 'Operations' and 'Technical Support'. Instead, it seems more logical to allocate development phases to existing Change Management or Release Management processes, which leaves a pure Operations Management process to be part of the IT Service Management process scope. Furthermore, by definition a process doesn't deal with infrastructure - as a consequence of the People, Process, Products distinction. For this reason we present a process domain titled Operations Management.

The classification of ICT Infrastructure Management under the heading 'Operations Management' in this book is to help those readers less familiar with the ITIL; it is also still common terminology to refer to these processes in this way. Metrics for ICT Infrastructure Management are:
- Number of plans signed off by the business
- Number of plans not ready for sign-off
- Delay from deployment plan
- Number of defects during deployment
- Number of serious or critical events per Managed Object (MO)
- Number of security events
- Number of job/script/backup failures
- Number of incidents as a result of operational changes
- Customer Satisfaction

8.2　Metrics for Tactical Service Management Processes

8.2.1 Service Level Management (G)

Metrics for Service Level Management are:
- Number of SLA targets missed
- Number of SLA targets threatened
- Percentage of SLAs that require changes
- Number of SLA reviews completed on time
- Number of SLA breaches caused by third party support contracts
- Service Delivery costs
- Number of services not covered by SLA
- Number of OLAs and Underpinning Contracts (UCs) not yet agreed upon
- Customer Satisfaction
- SLR -> SLA turnaround

8.2.2 Problem Management (H)

Please note that there is huge overlap between Problem Management and other tactical IT Service Management processes: where Problem Management has a focus on all problems, processes like Capacity Management and Availability Management focus on problems of a capacity or availability nature. This means that many metrics with a general nature could simply be translated to problems of a specific nature. We'll present the most important 'general' and 'specific' problems in the following paragraphs - leaving room for reapplication of general problems to specific areas.

Metrics for Problem Management are:
- Number of problems closed
- Number of incidents resolved by Known Errors
- Total number of incidents
- Total user downtime
- Number of RFCs raised by Problem Management
- Average number of open problems
- Average time to close a problem
- Percentage of incidents not linked to problems
- Number of problems that missed target resolution time
- Customer Satisfaction
- Top 5 categories of incidents reported for the period
- Number of incidents for which the solution is user training
- Cost of solving a problem

8.2.3 Financial Management for IT services (I)
Metrics for Financial Management are:
- Percentage of IT costs accounted for
- Number of changes made to charging algorithm
- Delay in production of financial report
- Delay in production of monthly forecast
- Percentage of accuracy of the last financial forecast
- Percentage of accuracy of financial forecast for the previous quarter
- Total Cost of Ownership (TCO) of IT
- Number of complaints regarding IT cost
- Number of questions regarding IT cost
- Customer Satisfaction

For ISO20000 purposes, the above is sufficient. Some organizations will wish to go further and become profit centres.

8.2.4 Capacity Management (J)
Metrics for Capacity Management are:
- Number of SLA breaches because of poor service performance
- Number of SLA breaches because of poor component
- Number of incidents as a result of poor performance and capacity
- Cost of production of Capacity Plan
- Number of unplanned purchases of performance related hardware
- Percentage of accuracy of plan of forecast expenditure
- Percentage of over-capacity of IT
- Percentage of CIs monitored for performance
- Customer Satisfaction
- Percentage overall Business Load of Expected Business Load

8.2.5 IT Service Continuity Management (K)

Metrics for IT Service Continuity Management are:
- Number of services not covered by IT Service Continuity (ITSC) plan
- Delay in ITSC plan completion/update
- Delay in ITSC test date
- Number of issues raised by last test still to be addressed
- Results from continuity awareness survey - Percentage of pass
- Number of issues identified this period that threaten the ITSC plan
- Number of targeted communications circulated
- Number of wrong entries in crisis control team directory
- Delay in preparedness of recovery site
- Customer Satisfaction

8.2.6 Availability Management (L)

Many Availability Management metrics find their origin in the 'incident lifecycle' - after all, incidents are one-on-one related to periods of un- or lesser availability. The incident lifecycle terminology in the core ITIL books is not completely consistent. Therefore an improved lifecycle is presented here, and used to find a large set of availability metrics. This includes the renaming of MTTR, from "Mean Time To Repair Downtime" to "Mean Time To Restore".

Metrics for Availability Management are:
- Downtime, Unavailability of services
- Unavailability of components
- Incident detection time
- Incident response time
- Incident repair time
- Incident recovery time
- Incident restoration time
- Incident resolution time
- MTBSI (Mean Time Between System Incidents)
- MTTR (Mean Time To Repair "downtime", Mean Time To Restore)
- Critical time failure
- Unavailability of third party services
- Unavailability of third party components
- Time used to resolve unavailable services
- Number of repeat failures

8.2.7 Security Management (M)

Metrics for Security Management are:
- Number of security related incidents
- Number of security related problems closed
- Number of Audit + Internal Review issues resolved
- Percentage of Reviews + Audits conducted on time
- Number of risks identified (warnings + new threats)
- Percentage of SLAs with explicit security specifications
- Percentage of UCs (Underpinning Contracts) with explicit security specifications

- Number of release security issues identified (back-outs/viruses etc.)
- Number of changes backed out as a result of security issues
- Security patch releasese speed

8.3 Metrics for strategic Service Management Processes

8.3.1 Business Perspective Metrics (N)

> The *goal* of *Business Perspective metrics* is *Quality of Experience* (QoE), a measure of business satisfaction aligned to business structures.

Quality of Experience can be achieved by:
- Aligning IT services with the needs of the business and its customers;
- Improving the quality of these IT services;
- Reducing the costs associated with providing these services.

Business Continuity Management describes the responsibilities and opportunities available to the business manager to improve what is, in most organizations, one of the key contributing services to business efficiency and effectiveness. This can be achieved by:
- Surviving change. IT infrastructure changes can impact the manner in which business is conducted or the continuity of business operations. It is important that busines managers take notice of these changes and ensure that steps are taken to safeguard the business from adverse side effects.
- Transformation of business practice through radical change helps to control IT and to integrate it with the business.
- Partnerships and outsourcing.

The Business Perspective comprises four processes:
1. Business Relationship Management
2. Supplier Relationship Management
3. Planning, Review and Development
4. Liaison, Education and Communication

The following three metrics are for the Business Perspective as a whole:
- Delivery cost per service
- Customer Satisfaction
- Business Knowledge of IT

The metrics below align to these processes, the sixteen Business Perspective metrics are made up of the three above and the thirteen that follow.

Business Relationship Management (N.1):
- Number of service complaints
- Number of outstanding actions against last Service Review

Supplier Relationship Management (N.2):
- Maximum incidents per supplier
- Percentage of contract suppliers conforming to standards like ISO20000
- Percentage supplier reviews completed on time
- Number of outstanding issues with suppliers

Managing Service Provision (N.3):
- Minimum Customer Satisfaction Score
- Number of incidents
- Customer Satisfaction

Planning, Review and Development (N.4):
- Number of issues identified in final Plan Review
- Number of plans signed off for implementation

Liaison, Education and Communication (N.5):
- Number of late actions in Communications Plan
- Percentage of IT staff not at optimal training level for their position

8.3.2 Continuous Service Improvement Programme (SIP) (O)

The Continuous Service Improvement Programme (SIP) covers all processes in an organization. It is a general rule with any complex system that changing too many things at the same time tends to lead to a negative result and makes it difficult to determine which change was responsible for which outcomes.

For this reason the SIP process usually prioritizes changes to processes based on how well the processes are performing and how important the performance is to the business.

ISO20000-1:2002 section 4.4 covers the actions required during the Continuous Improvement phase (the 'Act' of the 'Plan-Do-Check-Act' cycle). Using the results of the metrics outlined in this book, it is possible to identify the process or processes most in need of improvement. The impact of these processes can be discussed with the business and understood from their compliance with SLAs. The results of this consultative process can be used to produce a plan for the next cycle. As ISO20000 recommends, this plan is implemented and measured as a project. Once the project is complete, the effectiveness of the plan can be measured using the same metrics and SLAs that showed the deficiencies. The review of the plan thus provides a structure of improvement for the next SIP.

It can be seen that the SIP process itself follows exactly Deming's Plan-Do-Check-Act cycle of the implementation of other processes. This reveals the generalizing power of treating it as a process itself.

That is why we can also make a list of metrics for the SIP process. It can be tracked like any other process to make sure that real improvement is made. It is important that process owners make changes to the process that they are responsible for through the Change Management process so that these changes can be reflected in the SIP metrics as well as those that are part of

the formal SIP. Metrics for SIP are:
- Overall Customer Satisfaction
- Percentage of cost saving in last process SIP
- Percentage of processes overdue for SIP
- Number of outstanding approved actions that have not achieved their objective
- Number of outstanding actions in SIP Communications Plan
- Number of approved revisions to Service Management policies, plans and procedures
- Number of improvements carried out by process owners - outside SIP cycle
- Percentage of overall improvement since last benchmark
- Number of recommendations for improvement received from other Process Owners
- Number of changes requested for process improvement
- Number of SIPs on target

8.3.3 Risk Management (P)

Risk Management falls under the overall Company Risk Management policy. IT Risk decisions are based on business need. The balance between acceptable risk and cost cannot be made in isolation from this. Within Service Management, Risk Management is a component of a number of different processes:
- **Availability Management** - reduces the risk of downtime.
- **IT Service Continuity Management** - addresses the risk of catastrophic outage in the context of the Business Continuity Plan.
- **Change Management** - reduces the risk from uncontrolled changes.
- **Problem Management** - reduces the risk of repeated incidents leading to downtime or other damage.
- **Security Management** - reduces the risk of security events causing unacceptable downtime or other damage.
- **Incident Management** - reduces the risk of incidents causing extensive unavailability of business critical services.

The above risks are addressed insofar as the appropriate process metrics show the processes to be operating successfully. Within the Business Perspective, Risk Management and operational risk assessment must be aligned with business requirements.

Risk Management metrics are:
- Percentage of CIs covered by Business Impact Analysis
- Percentage of BIA documents not reviewed within required time
- Percentage of processes subject to Operational Risk Assesment (ORA)
- Number of incidents relating to risks not in ORA
- Percentage of incidents where occurrence is higher than predicted in ORA
- Percentage of CIs where downtime is greater than predicted in ORA
- Number of actions to reduce risk
- Number of newly identified risks
- Percentage of CIs not covered by Service Continuity Plan
- Number of meetings with suppliers, and internal process owners

8.3.4 Documentation Management (Q)

Documentation Management metrics are:

- Percentage of documents late for planned revision
- Percentage of documents not reviewed for one year
- Percentage of documents not accessed for one year
- Number of outstanding requests for document changes
- Number of documents not removed after end of life
- Number of SLAs missing documentation
- Number of incomplete Service Management policies and plans
- Number of incompatibilities between specific plans and the service management plan
- Number of documentation related incidents
- Customer Satisfaction

8.3.5 Competence, Awareness and Training (CAT) (R)

CAT metrics are:

- Number of late actions from Awareness Campaign
- Number of job descriptions missing specific competence requirement
- Percentage of IT staff with professional industry recognition
- Mean Percentage of shortfall from optimal level of training
- Percentage of staff with a signed Personal Development Plan
- Percentage of IT staff not at optimal training level for their position
- Percentage of staff not meeting minimum competence
- Percentage of staff with overdue actions against their development plan
- Percentage of awareness in organization
- Percentage of IT staff turnover
- Number of outstanding job requisitions
- Number of staff with no defined role or responsibility

8.4 Metrics for Programme and Project Management (S)

Programme and Project Management metrics are:

- Number of milestones missed
- Total project delay this month
- Number of new project issues
- Number of project issues resolved this month
- Number of risks identified
- Critical Path delay
- Escalation
- Number of project meetings slipped
- Estimated percentage of certainty of meeting project end-date on budget
- Customer Satisfaction
- Number of outstanding actions from steering meetings

9 Integrating Metrics

Many attempts have been made in the past to improve the measurement of business processes. Many too have been tried in IT. Mostly they have concentrated on development activities where metrics are fairly mature.

A number of recent changes has brought measurement of other areas into sharper focus. Corporate Governance has become an important issue, certainly for large international companies, but, increasingly for smaller companies as well. Service Management initiatives have also stressed the importance of measurement. The ITIL, ISO20000, COBIT, Six Sigma and eTOM all are devoted towards using metrics to ensure that processes are performing as they have been designed to and to enable a probably effective process improvement Programme to be put in place.

These initiatives have taken different approaches and started from different views of IT. Consequently the results are not directly compatible. This chapter considers how best to work towards integrating metrics from different schemes.

The **objectives** behind the production of metrics determine their structure and usefulness. A set of metrics designed to ensure good governance will not necessarily assist with the improvement of technical delivery processes or the reduction of cost to IT.

All is not lost though! A set of metrics designed to control Service Management processes, enable cost reduction and process improvement can be used to provide governance information.

9.1 Governance

General business governance has become an important topic in recent years. A number of initiatives to improve Corporate Governance have been undertaken and some have become law in various parts of the world (Sarbanes-Oxley in the US, Basel II in Europe, and King II in South Africa). All of these have in common a strong financial basis. The control of and proper use and disposal of assets are part of the focus. At the core of the ITIL Service Support and Service Delivery processes are the Configuration and Change Management processes. ISO20000 makes the central control function of these processes even more specific.

Whilst Configuration and Change Management are central to the IT Service Management processes they also, as a side-effect, provide life-cycle management of IT related assets.

Sarbanes-Oxley requires strict division between auditors of an area and those responsible for the area - this is also a requirement of ISO20000.

Checklists to enable Governance levels to be checked against IT Service Management controls and Sarbanes-Oxley requirements have been produced by the Committee of Sponsoring Organizations of the Treadway Commission (COSO) and these can be used to check the maturity level of governance put in place using, for example, ISO20000.

9.2 ITIL - ISO20000 (BS15000)

ISO20000 (and previously BS15000 in the UK, AS8018 in Australia and SANS15000 in South Africa) contains two parts. Part 1 is the Specification for Service Management that includes a checklist for what is absolutely required: the 'shall' of implementation. Part 2 is the Code of Practice for Service Management and includes a checklist of what companies ought to implement as well: the 'should' of implementation.

Most implementers will, ultimately, wish to comply with both parts. In fact, the standard does not cover all ITIL processes or functions, it does not include ICT Infrastructure Management or Application Management, for example, and is a minimum quality level for IT Operations. So, almost all companies will exceed the standard in many areas.

Though there are many other requirements, simply in terms of metrics, the standard requires that the following processes and functions are properly measured:
- Management System
  - Continuous Service Improvement Programme (8.3.2)
  - Risk Management (8.3.3)
  - Documentation requirements (8.3.4)
  - Competence, Awareness and Training (8.3.5)
- Service Delivery Processes
  - Capacity Management (8.2.4)
  - Availability and Service Continuity Management (8.2.5 and 8.2.6)
  - Service Level Management (8.2.1)
  - Service Reporting (10.4)
  - Information Security Management (8.2.7)
  - Budgeting and Accounting (Financial Management) for IT Services (8.2.3)
- Control Processes
  - Configuration Management (7 and 8.1.3)
  - Change Management (8.1.4)
- Release Process
  - Release Management (8.1.5)
- Resolution Process
  - Incident Management (8.1.1)
  - Problem Management (8.2.2)
- Relationship Processes
  - Business Relationship Management (8.3.1)
  - Supplier Management (8.3.1)

The relevant chapters in this book are marked above.

9.3 eTOM

The enhanced Telecom Operations Map (eTOM) is used by many Telecoms companies as a service delivery platform, based on network management standards and using business process methods. The TeleManagement Forum provides many white papers describing eTOM as well as a detailed matrix showing the relationship between ITIL and eTOM.

The mapping of ITIL to eTOM is defined in detail by the document GB921L[1] produced by the above forum. It is important to be aware that the terminology, scope and definitions in eTOM and ITIL are different so, though it can be used to support eTOM, ITIL is not directly or easily mapped to eTOM, so this document is a guideline only and does not recognize much of ITIL.

From a very high level, though, the alignment can be seen as shown in table 9.1.

eTOM	ITIL
Service Quality Management	Availability
Customer QoS/SLA Management	Service Level
Problem Handling	Incident
Customer Interface Management	Service Desk
Service Problem/Resource	Trouble Problem
Service Configuration and Activation/Resource Provisioning	Configuration

Table 9.1 Correspondence between eTOM and ITIL

It is important to note that many terms that are used in both systems are defined differently! 'Service' and, as can be seen above, 'problem', mean different things.

From the point of view of metrics, the approach taken in this book can be extended to fit in with eTOM processes, that operate at a higher level.

9.4 COBIT

COBIT is the auditing standard used to test IT compliance with legislation (e.g. Sarbanes-Oxley). COBIT's control objectives are quite closely aligned to the ITIL. During the design of COBIT, ITIL Best Practice was used to define categories, so COBIT control objectives are designed to produce a good fit with the ITIL - and, by extension, ISO20000.

As with the ITIL, the starting point is a Service Catalogue against which service delivery can be measured. SLA measures and process metrics provide detailed evidence of how IT Service Management is controlled. If an organization is using, or intends to use, COBIT as an audit mechanism, it is useful to benchmark the process design and metrics using the COBIT defined control objectives during the implementation of Service Management processes. This ensures that particular choices of metrics for the organization will match COBIT audit requirements in advance of implementation.

If we consider the High Level Control Objectives for monitoring:
- **M1-** Monitor the Processes
- **M2-** Assess Internal Control Adequacy
- **M3-** Obtain Independent Assurance
- **M4-** Provide for Independent Audit

1. http://www.tmforum.org/browse.asp?catID=2024&linkID=29248 - this is the direct link, eTOM is maintained by www.tmforum.org and this link allows the document to be downloaded for free by members, but at substantial cost for non-members.

We can see that the ISO20000 structure aligns with this. The metrics defined and discussed in this book directly satisfy Control Objective M1.

The above is one example of how the mapping operates. Apart from the consideration of metrics, the detail mapping between COBIT and ITIL is contained in books devoted to the topic, for example the itSMF-NL 'IT Governance - A Pocket Guide Based on COBIT' is recommended for the next level of detail.[2]

Some people have seen COBIT as a replacement for ITIL. It is not a replacement, but complimentary. COBIT is a highly stable method of design and is extremely helpful to IT audit. It is best seen as a framework to support IT auditors - the best gain is found by designing your metric system with both Audit and Operations in mind. It is worth mentioning, though, that COBIT has a large number of metrics used by audit and it is wise to be familiar with those to be sure that any new metrics that are designed are aligned to these so that the audit process is enhanced.

9.5 Six Sigma

Six Sigma works as a business process model with an aim to reduce 'defects' to within a certain fault ranges ('sigma'). In order to do this, metrics are required through which 'defects' can be identified.

The metrics developed for IT Service Management in this book are compatible with the Six Sigma approach. Once the metrics have been benchmarked and a history developed, a 'defect' can be seen as a failure to meet an agreed metric objective. This aligns the two systems and allows Six Sigma goals to be made meaningful in an IT Service Management context.

Six Sigma moves away from the approach taken here where average performance of processes against metrics are considered. Six Sigma emphasizes the importance of reducing single defects. It is wise, therefore, to have the IT Service Management framework in place for some time, six months or a year, probably, to go through a number of cycles of the SIP and refine both the processes and the metrics that measure them before exposing them to the rigour of Six Sigma.

It is important to realize that Six Sigma, with its origins in manufacturing, is helpful in managing the process of reducing defects, but is not going to help much in designing metrics for Service Management. If there is a Six Sigma project existing in a company, there is a danger that the 'tail wags the dog'. This can be avoided by putting in Service Management metrics in place first, as recommended here, and putting them through a process improvement cycle, then working to fit the results into the Six Sigma framework.

It is also worth noting that the high quality levels in Six Sigma can be expensive. Even Motorola realized that the cost of quality was very high and started reducing the quality level to improve profitability. It is important to use common sense, rather than idealism, in setting Six Sigma targets. The balance between cost and quality is not easy to establish.

---

2 There's also an interesting paper on OGC's website, "Aligning COBIT ®, ITIL® and ISO 17799 for Business Benefit" at http://www.itil.co.uk/includes/ITIL-COBiT.pdf.

10   Implementing Metrics

It is possible to measure things over which you have no control - the amount of light emitted from the sun, for example. That may be interesting and might help understand why things are as they are, but it does not help control anything!

To control a business or IT process, the process must be defined and followed. In other words, it must be implemented. The metric must be designed so that the information required can be gathered from the operating process and the people working the process must understand what influence they have on improving the metric as well as having some incentive to make the improvement.

If metrics are introduced in isolation, the best that can be expected is that there might be some interesting figures. That is all.

This section considers what must be done in order for metrics to be introduced and then be useful as a control mechanism to move the organization in the direction required by management.

If you don't know where you wish to go, then you can't do much to get there! It is necessary to have a Management System (as it is described in ISO20000) that knows where it wants to go. That is, it has a Service Management policy, objectives and plans.

10.1   Activities

In order to be successful in IT Service Management, an organization must have senior management commitment to achieve that success. This is described by ITIL as having an 'Executive Sponsor'. Without this any attempts will have limited success and, ultimately, be frustrating and ineffective for those making them.

The first activity, therefore, is to communicate the benefits, costs and implementation requirements to Senior Management. If this communication is successful in convincing Senior Management of the need for IT Service Management then a Management System will be put in place as described in section 3 'Requirements for a management system' (ISO20000-1:20000).

Once this has been done, the requirements for metrics to monitor processes as they are put into place will be generally understood, as it is part of the ITIL Foundations Course.

At this early stage, it is ideal if the principle of a consistent, simple and comparable set of metrics is put in place across all processes. This is the approach suggested in this book. It has the benefit of simplifying the job for process owners who have plenty of work implementing the People - Process - Technology side of process implementation.

Ideally, metrics are designed into processes as the processes themselves are designed. Much has been written about process design. Much has been made of it being important not to be 'tool driven'. It is true that processes must suit the requirements of an organization. Few are complete 'green field' sites. So a set of standard processes, such as those supplied by consultants or supported 'out of the box' by various tools, will need to be adapted to suit local conditions. Designing new processes from the ground up is a lengthy process in itself and often a thankless one as it delivers a set of documents, not any improvement to the organization!

If the metrics in this book are taken with a standard top-level process design for a particular process and used as a template, along with information as to what actually is supported by the selected tool (or tools that are likely to be selected), then the process is made simpler and quicker. All that is necessary is to find exceptions where the standard process will not suit the organization and, where it is the best solution, making changes to fit these exceptions. Thus the majority of the process and metrics can be used 'as is', with a few well defined exceptions.

Naturally such a design process will not produce perfect processes! No other design process will either. The SIP exists to refine the original design, so there is no need to fear that the organization will be landed forever with a sub-optimal solution. Quite the reverse, the organization will have a quick, easy to implement solution that can be refined over time in the light of genuine business need. Exactly what ITIL requires.

10.2 Critical Success Factors

The top CSF is a committed management team - a Management System, including policies and a framework to enable the effective management and implementation of all IT services (ISO20000-1:2—2 Section 3 Objective).

For this system to be effective, it is vital that a good communication plan is put in place and followed.

Once this is in place, the contents and recommendations of this book can be added to the Service Management Policy. For example:

> *"The policy for implementing metrics for processes in organization ABC is that a set of approximately ten metrics is designed per process, in such a way that the effectiveness of these metrics can be measured and the design method used is consistent across all processes. This is to ensure that process maturity and improvement can be compared using the results of the metrics."*

In practice this then means that, when creating or changing a process, the process owner will consult other process owners to check that the metrics will be consistent and allow that comparison. This discussion will include the question of how to baseline the metrics in a realistic fashion. A common practice can be developed. This might be, for example, for each process to be put in place and run as a beta implementation for three months, with the standard set of metrics in place. The average of the best three weeks during that period is then taken as the baseline with the target figures being a percentage of improvement against that baseline.

The above would be a pragmatic approach that could easily be changed if it was found too easy or too much of a stretch for particular processes.

Once the above approach has been taken, metrics are likely to be usable and to provide valuable management information. A list of further Critical Success Factors follows:
• Supporting Management System
• Good Communications Plan
• Consistent process design
• Consistent metric design
• Consistent monitoring and collection method
• Collection and monitoring independent of process owners
• Metrics follow design principles outlined in Chapter 8

10.3 Possible problems

Too few metrics or too many metrics or simply badly designed metrics can all produce spectacularly bad results.

The ISO20000 standard puts great emphasis on the 'Management System' that supports Service Management. This is important. If metrics are not part of the individual objectives of process owners and those working in IT supporting the various processes, then they have limited power to influence behaviour. If the Management System is not in place to put sufficient management attention onto metrics, they also lack force.

If metrics are not seen as an important way in which management measures and rewards individual effort then there is no incentive for individuals to make particular effort to make the metrics better. It is vitally important, therefore, that the Management System is in place and the importance of the metrics to management is communicated and reinforced through regular reviews as well as making them part of individual objectives. If this is not done then there may be some initial enthusiasm, but, after a time, attention will not be paid to them and delivery will deteriorate.

If metrics do not comply with some of the design criteria mentioned in the early chapters (SMART, KISS) they may not work either. If a metric is not achievable, or is perceived as not being achievable, people may well give up trying to achieve it, thinking that, if failure is inevitable there is little point in trying to make it a little bit less of a failure as that effort is unlikely to bring much reward!

The criteria of measurability and establishing realistic goals can also pose challenges in implementing metrics. For example, if average time taken in call handling by any support team is a metric, then the time spent on each call by each support member must be captured accurately. When this is not enabled by a tool and needs to be captured manually outside of the tool, it takes further effort to record. Hence while implementing metrics, considerable effort may be required in customizing the tool to enable data capture.

Metrics and the implementation of them, can appeal to the technocrat or 'analytical' personality. They appear in mathematical format and many complex graphs can be produced showing all sorts of different views of the data. This has a number of dangers.

Firstly, what is important is simplicity in presentation - it is better to see what is going well, or not, quickly, than to know exactly what is going wrong to several decimal places! Finding out exactly what the problem is is part of the resolution process, not part of the identification of the problem. Section 10.4.1 goes deeper into the subject of presenting metrics.

Secondly, though metrics are technical in implementation and presentation, they are actually measuring what people do. What people do and how they react to incentives or pressure are soft management questions, not technocratic ones. Treating people as if they are some sort of machine (as occurred in the '60s with 'Time and Motion' studies) can answer some interesting questions - but often at the cost of alienating people. We are individuals and respond well to being treated as such. If our manager takes an interest in us and measures how well we do our job using both metrics (as an objective source of evidence) and personal knowledge, then we are likely to respond well to suggestions.

If we are judged only by what percentage of calls we answer in less than so many minutes, then we are likely to treat our job mechanically, not give of our best and, with the consequent low morale, be prepared to change jobs easily. The result for the organization is high turn over, poor morale and, as a result, poor service to customers.

10.3.1 Resistance to change

Resistance to change is an important factor in human behaviour, as is **inertia**. It is important for those setting up and running processes to be aware of both of these. This is well discussed in many other places so is only briefly introduced here. The point being made is that with metrics the 'rubber hits the road'. Notional compliance can be given by organizations and employees (and indeed Management Sponsors!) without there being genuine adoption. Metrics can reveal this very starkly and become the target of resistance. Hence they need to be well defined and agreed upon so that they can be defended.

The second, inertia, can only be remedied by constant management vigilance. If process meetings become boring, time-consuming affairs where little of importance is discussed then it is only natural that they will be devalued in importance. They will then not be taken seriously. People will be sent to stand-in for principals and the real work of monitoring and improving the processes will not be done.

This can happen if meetings are held too often or if decisions are not made and then followed up from the meetings. It might help to view the matter of monitoring and improving processes as a process itself that can be monitored for effectiveness just like any other process. It is after all part of the SIP (Service Improvement Plan).

Subversion of the process is unlikely to be consciously deliberate, though that is possible. If metrics are not complete in time for the meeting and this is allowed to occur regularly, for example, then this can be a way of hiding bad news until something can be done about it. Or avoiding the resolution of a problem that might have a serious business impact.

In order to prevent these problems, it is important that meetings to discuss metrics are formally documented so that missing or incomplete metrics form part of the minutes circulated to all parties and are not simply brushed under the carpet.

If metrics are made too difficult to understand or gather, they will, naturally, create antagonism and resistance. If a particular metric or metrics tend to be missing or incomplete, it is probably wise to have a separate meeting. This will discuss these particular metrics with a view to either changing them, if that is appropriate, or improving the understanding of how they work, why they are being collected and what can be done to make the collection more effective.

Metrics are revealing of process operation in a way in which discussion, observation and other informal methods are not. If processes are not being adhered to for any reason, this is likely to become apparent through metrics. So, if the matter of resistance to change has not been resolved in some part of the organization, the symptom is likely to be difficulties in reporting or gathering metrics, or poor results from the metrics.

For these reasons, it is important not to see these problems reflecting on the people reporting the metrics. It is all too easy to try to put in place actions to solve something that is not the problem! Rather, if a trend appears, where it looks as if the intent of the metrics programme is being subverted, it is important to find the root cause. This may be a boundary or interface between a department or process that has been working towards ITIL and one that has not. It might be a change in the business that has made an existing process no longer effective. It might simply be new staff left out by the induction and training process. What is important is for this to be investigated and a remedy put in place.

The tensions that result from these forms of resistance can be severe and can have a strong negative effect on morale and proper operation of the Business Processes. It is important to keep the ITIL Executive Sponsor aware of the difficulties so that senior management attention can be applied before a major crisis develops.

Remember, if you see the 'engine temperature' warning in your car heading for the Red Line, then stop the car and deal with the problem! Blaming the temperature gauge will not help.

10.3.2 Metrics and MOC (Management of Change)

Change Management manages changes that are to be made in the organization. The Management of Change (MOC) is the term used for the management challenge of ensuring that organizational and operational change is absorbed by the organization and people.

Human Resources provide assistance to management, including the provision of training courses, in the Management of Change. Briefly, the process involves communicating the corporate and management vision of the organization and why the change is necessary to all employees who are to be affected by the change.

This communication involves dealing with particular human factors, or 'soft', issues that relate to the change. Answering such questions as 'Will I keep my job?', 'Will the new objectives that have been added to my job mean that I will be paid at a higher grade?', 'What training will I receive to help me in the transition to the new job and responsibilities?'.

Since the ultimate objective of implementing IT Service Management metrics is to have employee objectives aligned to them, it is clear that, to be managed well, the Management of Change must be taken into account. The discipline is important to management as well as it ensures that the detailed working out of the changes from a vision of a smoothly functioning operation where people are measured by how well they perform in improving the functioning of the process that they are responsible for or help deliver to actual changes in day to day working practices.

Some of this communication may seem to some to be a matter of 'cosmetics'. Indeed this term is sometimes applied to changes that only affect day-to-day personal factors. It is important to realize that, if badly handled, these apparently trivial factors can lead to strong employee resistance and to the possible failure of the project! It is unwise to underestimate the importance of making sure that 'people factors' are taken into account when planning changes.

Until process thinking becomes standard in an organization, it is important to help employees understand that the process is what requires improving and attention, not the individual. Individual growth and improvement are separate, and important, factors that are independent of process improvement. If this is not understood then great anxiety can be caused when process failure or graphs of metrics appear to show some departments 'failing'.

Once the negative impressions have been dealt with, it is possible to engender friendly competition between different process owners and their teams (direct reports or virtual teams) in a positive contribution to process improvement.

10.3.3 Consequences of Metrics (The Law of Unintended Consequences: Machiavellian Metrics)

Metrics do not make things happen by themselves. They are part of a Management Framework and have the function of informing Management of the current state of affairs and how it has changed from previously.

Part of the problem is that the measure becomes based not on behaviour that assists the business, but simply on that which satisfies the metric. When a tax on windows was established in 1696, it seemed a reasonable progressive tax. The richer the householder the bigger the house and more expensive glass windows there would be, so the richest would pay more tax than the poorest. It worked up to a point, but you can still, in England, see many houses with bricked-up windows, with dim interiors as a result just to avoid the tax. Not only that, but the tax turned windows into status symbols with the very rich building manor houses with the maximum of windows. Some had windows built over structural walls, of no use but to attract tax and status! Neither of these effects were intended or thought of when the tax was invented.

> **Quote from "IT Infrastructure Library practices in small IT units"[3], 1995:**
> The number of calls to the Help Desk is one of the most popular, and yet one of the hardest measures to interpret. It is a very popular measurement, primarily because it is very easy to collect. But it is very hard to interpret; since nobody rings the Help Desk because they want to but because they need to. Thus the measurement depends on other variables.
>
> Possible reasons for an increase in calls can be manifold and contradictory. For example:
> - a bad help desk might attract more calls, because users have to keep calling until their problem is resolved
> - a good help desk might receive more calls because users, encouraged by a good service, are using it more often
> - just letting users know that there is one central point of contact can, in itself, increase the number of calls.
> - a new release or change of software will attract more calls
> - any change of staff or working practices will result in more calls because users are not so familiar with the service
> - the work may be seasonal, so that less familiar parts of the IT system are being used at certain times of the year
> - there may be a problem with the delivery of the service, such as:
>   - changes not being properly tested
>   - software getting out of step across a distributed system
>   - network or hardware going down.
>
> All this shows that metrics are not independent, and not easy to interpret; just because something is easy to count does not mean that it should become a key ITSM measurement.

Another well-known example that has affected all of us is the use of 'call duration' as a metric in customer call centres. Operators are, because of this measure, obsessed with 'closing the call' rather than dealing with the needs of the customer. Often, before the matter is properly resolved they will ask, 'can I close this call now' and even go as far as to encourage you to open a new call about the same matter, rather than keep a valid call open and decrease their closing efficiency. This approach does not lead to Customer Satisfaction!

In the above example, it is clear that there is value to the organization in not having calls open for long periods. It is also important to customers that their calls are dealt with promptly. The mistake is to make this the sole or most important measure. There are two clear ways of dealing with this particular difficulty. One is to measure repeat calls on the same subject. If these are common, then the call closing metric is causing unhelpful behaviour and it will become important to make sure that people do not open new calls on the same, or a similar, subject.

Alternatively, Customer Satisfaction surveys can identify that customers are not happy when asked to close calls simply for the convenience of the operator and the level of satisfaction of customers can be made a more important metric.

---

3 This book will be renewed in the current ITIL® Refresh project. The new title will be: ITIL small-scale implementation.

The prioritizing of metrics enables such requirements to be fine-tuned over time. When operators know that Customer Satisfaction is the important measure, they will not insist on closing calls, but rather make sure that the customer is happy with the resolution before asking if a call can be closed. If this leads, over time, to call duration becoming unacceptably long, the priorities can again be adjusted.

The alternative, taken in this book, is to employ the logic that Machiavelli recommended in human relationships. That is to consider what behaviour is likely when given a particular goal. A good test is 'What would I do, if I had this as my objective!'. If this is different from what the true objective of the metric is, then a second, balancing, metric can be employed. Thus, 'call duration' can be balanced with 'customer satisfaction'.

This is one of the driving forces behind the choice of metrics in this book. We will all try to do what we can to satisfy the objectives of the organization, but our main objective is to do well ourselves. If our metrics encourage us to do things that are good for us, but not for the organization, then it is the metric design that is at fault - not us!

The examples above are fairly well known. In real life, the unintended consequences of metrics being put into place tend to be subtler. It is important to check the actual operation of metrics in a process to make sure that they are measuring genuine process variables. And that these relate to the service being provided, and are not just bureaucratic intrusions into the job people are doing! Balancing metrics against each other, as recommended here, is a good start, but it is no substitute for actually going to meet the people working on the process and finding out what they do and how the metric impinges on that. Checking the usefulness and accuracy of metrics is probably a good objective to add to the Service Improvement Plan.

10.4 Service Reporting

> The fundamental **goal** of **Service Reporting** is to communicate the message effectively. This objective is achieved through clarity and visual impact.
> "A picture is worth a thousand words."

Many organizations have their own standard reporting requirements. The aim of any report is to make the data clear, unambiguous and easy to understand. A considerable number of different graphical methods have been used to achieve this.

Many visual reporting packages provide coloured pie charts, bar charts, spider diagrams, linear graphs as well as representations of three-dimensional representations of data. A set of data can easily be represented in any of these formats. So much so that there is a danger that the attractive graphical representations can be given more attention than the message! The aim must always be for simplicity and clarity rather than for aesthetic appearance. The rule of thumb is:
• Pie chart for component comparison
• Bar graph for item comparison
• Column chart for time series comparison
• Frequency distribution in line chart
• Correlation comparison in scatter chart

The reporting also needs to be appropriate for the level. A report summarizing a large amount of underlying detail is best understood if presented graphically. A report for a particular process manager may well work better as tabular data so that particular detail can be examined to produce an action plan. An appropriate division is into the levels of increasing detail from Strategic to Tactical to Operational.

Metrics reports have three important views:

1. **The historical view** - How have the processes fared over the past number of reporting periods? This enables short-term blips to be understood in context, avoiding panic actions when the underlying situation is acceptable. It also enables dangerous trends to be spotted in advance, even if current results appear good, so that action can be taken in advance of business affecting situations developing.
2. **The view relative to other processes** - How is the organization as a whole progressing? Which process is performing best relative to the others? How are the processes performing relative to benchmark results from other organizations? This view enables fine-tuning of the continuous improvement plan.
3. **The current snapshot view** - What particular issues have occurred over the past period? How serious are they? What can be done to prevent them from occurring again?

Whilst many reports can be produced automatically from Service Management or Reporting toolsets, it is important that manual checking for reasonableness is done. The ISO20000 auditing principle applies to the production and checking of reports. This ought to be done by a separate person from the person responsible for the service being reported. All reports ought to be reassessed for need every six-months (or quarterly) and discontinued if not needed.

ISO20000 states the objective of Service Reporting as:

> *'To produce agreed, timely, reliable, accurate reports for informed decision making and effective communication'. It further states that there shall be a clear description of each service report including its identity, purpose, audience and details of the data source (ISO20000-1: 2004).*

Regular reports are in danger of being overlooked simply because the format appears the same. For this reason it is often more useful to produce exception reports. That is, when a process, or processes achieve high levels of improvement or show sudden decreases it is worth highlighting this in a special communication along with the activities that have led to the improvement or that have been scheduled to rectify the decrease. Simply reporting that everything is on-track, as usual, invites no action and does not add much value.

Distributing paper reports is expensive, time consuming and they are often not read. Remember the reply to a survey on the usefulness of reports, saying 'Please keep them coming, my five year old daughter finds them excellent for drawing on'. It is probably wiser to put the reports onto an internal web-site where they are generally accessible and to distribute an e-mail describing the exceptions. This way, interested parties can see the most recent reports when required but are only directly involved when there is a particular need.

Whether distributing paper or web-site reports, in both cases meetings with key stakeholders should be scheduled regularly to ensure key metric performance data is discussed, agreed & actioned. If solely left for people to access when they need it, the data will be in danger of being ignored.

Section 10.4.1 contains reports produced for all processes in one week as well as showing a three-month graph comparing the level of improvement in different metrics.

10.4.1 The presentation of metrics

Presentation of information to management must be clear, highlighting areas requiring attention and avoiding too much detail. The aim is to assist decision making and communicate results of previous decisions.

The metrics in this book have been designed so that each process is measured in a fairly similar way, there is a Customer Satisfaction metric to balance a set of single dimensional mainly technical metrics. Many of the targets make no sense in the abstract. They only make sense when either measured against benchmarks (or baselines) from other organizations or when measured against past performance.

Past performance, usually over the previous quarter, in a highly seasonal industry compared to the same months the previous year, is a good guide to whether performance has improved or got worse. Naturally it is not enough to see the measure and decide that the process has got worse (or better) because there are likely to be many other factors at work that can produce a temporary blip. However a trend, taken over the previous six months should even these out and give a clearer picture of actual performance.

What is of interest in managing overall direction is not the mass of detail found in the metrics, but a comparison between processes against the trend over the past few months. A few examples of how to display this information follow with explanations of how to interpret them. There is no space in this book to cover the algorithms necessary to produce this consolidation, so only the results are shown.

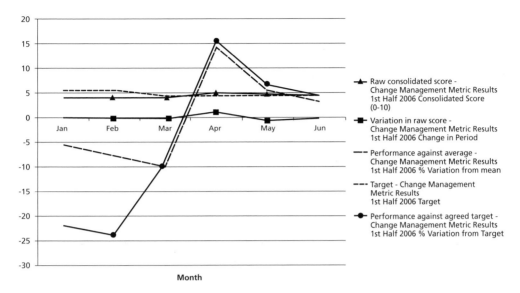

Change Management Metric Results 1st Half 2006

Raw consolidated score - Change Management Metric Results 1st Half 2006 Consolidated Score (0-10)

Variation in raw score - Change Management Metric Results 1st Half 2006 Change in Period

Performance against average - Change Management Metric Results 1st Half 2006 % Variation from mean

Target - Change Management Metric Results 1st Half 2006 Target

Performance against agreed target - Change Management Metric Results 1st Half 2006 % Variation from Target

Figure 10.1 Sample Showing Change Management Metrics

In the above graph, the metrics for Change Management have been consolidated into a single number for each month. This number includes all the metrics, weighted by the priority agreed between management and the process owner expressed so that it can be compared to other processes. The Service Level Management Process has, as we know, quite different metrics, but its graph would appear similar to the above.

To interpret the the three lines:

- From the line showing **the raw consolidated score,** we can see that the process has been close to a score of 5 for this period.
- The **performance against the agreed target -** the best comparison between processes. After a disappointing start, we see that we improved in March but have dropped off since then.
- **Performance against average** shows how Change Management has done against its average peformance for the period - this shows the same big improvement in March with a drop off later.
- There's also a line showing the **variation in the raw score**.
- The **target** line shows the target was changed during the period - it was placed too high to be achievable, but it has since been overtaken.

Further investigation would be needed to find out why this has all occurred. However very quick inspection shows us that, on the whole, Change Management has improved, even though the last two months have not been as good as April. This would be a lot more difficult to establish from looking at all the detail of the metrics for these months.

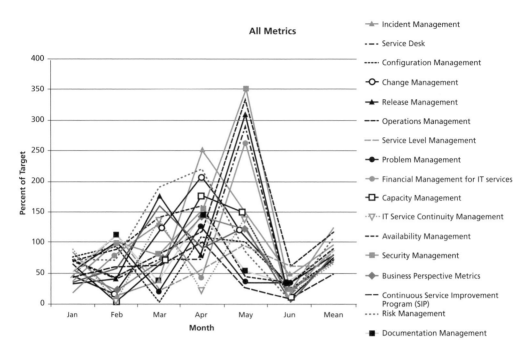

Figure 10.2 All Consolidate Metrics

The above graph shows all the metrics on one sheet. Even though we have consolidated them into one number it is still confusing. We can see that Release Management has done worst overall (showing the lowest mean) and the SIP has done best. Most interesting, though, is that build up to the peak of performance in May and the fall in June. It is likely that this company has quite a strong seasonal trend. To get the overall picture, a 'radar' or 'spider web' diagram gives a better picture of the order of the processes.

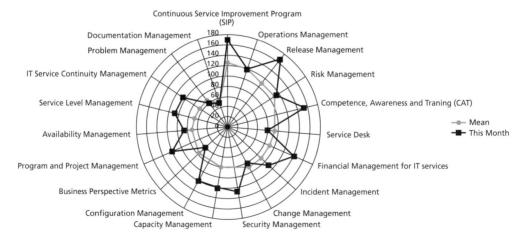

Figure 10.3 Spider web diagram of the average over the past six months

From this diagram, looking at the *pale gray* line, giving the mean, we can easily see that Documentation is the biggest problem area, whilst, fortunately, the SIP is doing best of all - so there is hope for things doing well in the future.

This puts the *dark gray* line into perspective. In a real example it would be unlikely that there would be quite so much variation, but we can easily see that the five processes that have done less well this month are: Service Desk, Change Management, the Business Perspective, Problem and Documentation Management. It would make sense for the SIP to concentrate on these, particularly the final two, that have also done badly over the entire period relative to their targets.

11 Continuous improvement with metrics

> 'Now! Now!' cried the Queen. 'Faster! Faster!' And they went so fast that at last they seemed to skim through the air, hardly touching the ground with their feet, till suddenly, just as Alice was getting quite exhausted, they stopped, and she found herself sitting on the ground, breathless and giddy.
> The Queen propped her up against a tree, and said kindly, 'You may rest a little now.'
>
> Alice looked round her in great surprise. 'Why, I do believe we've been under this tree the whole time! Everything's just as it was!'
>
> 'Of course it is,' said the Queen, 'what would you have it?'
>
> 'Well, in our country,' said Alice, still panting a little, 'you'd generally get to somewhere else - if you ran very fast for a long time, as we've been doing.'
>
> 'A slow sort of country!' said the Queen. 'Now, here, you see, it takes all the running you can do, to keep in the same place.'
>
> *Through the Looking Glass, by Lewis Carroll*

The Red Queen from Alice in Wonderland said that in her country you had to keep running just to stay in the same place. This is important to consider: organizations need to improve continuously nowadays in order to maintain their positions. There are many management philosophies advocating this Continuous Service Improvement approach, from Deming's *Plan Do Check Act cycle* to Six Sigma's *Define Measure Analyze Improve and Control "cookbook"*.

All these philosopies have one thing in common: without measuring process outcomes they won't be able to truly change a company's culture and results. How should the goals of metrics be tightened to ever-changing organizations? How should metrics themselves be changed as processes and organizations mature?

If a process always achieves 9/10 of its metrics, but fails on 1 then attention has to be paid to what is special about that one and how it can be broken down into its components and measured in more detail.

Recently a large organization dismantled its reporting department, consisting of over a hundred people, when it became clear that not only were the reports it produced not being used to make important business decisions, but they duplicated information that was already easy to obtain elsewhere. The danger is clear, like all bureaucracies, if the production of reports is allowed to exist as a separate function, uncoupled from the Continuous Service Improvement Programme (SIP) and not measured for usefulness and efficiency, it can consume far more resources than an organization can reasonably wish to be allocated to the function.

It is important to understand exactly what actions can be taken if a particular metric delivers a result that is outside the desired range. If there is no particular action then it is better not to collect the metric. It costs money to collect information and this is justified only if the information is useful.

If metrics reported to Service Management go into too much detail then there is a danger that changes, even quite small ones, to the process itself, as will be required by the operation of the SIP, will make the metric impossible to collect. To avoid this, metrics need to measure fundamental parts of the process that contribute to its effectiveness. It is possible to measure several hundred metrics using Service Management tools, but many of them are not useful for making decisions that help improve the process - they are measurable but not meaningful.

It is worth looking at the objectives that the metrics satisfy. If you look at Service Management from a top-down perspective, the Business identifies a Vision of where it wishes to go and what it needs to do to get there. This enables a Strategy to be developed which, in turn, defines Plans, Policies and Objectives which determine what is to be done. Understanding this perspective makes it easier to see why certain metrics make no sense in terms of the overall company direction, whilst others are extremely important. It is not always possible to develop metrics in exactly this manner, but this is a worthwhile sanity check before a set of metrics is deployed.

This book has tried to provide you with a list of these kinds of meaningful metrics, each of them being aligned to a clear process goal and objective. Also, guidelines on how to create metrics on your own have been provided, along with tips on how and when to use them, as well as tips on presenting them and comparing them to each other. In the appendices that follow, all metrics provided in chapter ten will be explained further. These metrics are meant to help you get started, but may of course be adjusted to all specific needs of your organization.

A   Metrics for Incident Management

The primary **goal** of the Incident Management process is to restore normal service operation as quickly as possible (and agreed) and minimize the adverse impact on business operations, thus ensuring that the best possible levels of service quality and availability are maintained. 'Normal service operation' is defined here as a service operation within Service Level Agreement (SLA) limits.

(OGC ITIL Best Practice for Service Support)

Mission Statement:
To minimize the impact of service disruptions to the business by restoring that service through effective management of incidents.

Process owner: Incident Manager

Metric Objective: To prevent a breach in agreed service levels by ensuring the timely resolution of incidents.

Metric:	Percentage of incidents resolved by 1st Line Support {%incidents}
Description:	How many incidents require no escalation to second line support.
Specification:	A count of incidents that require no escalation.
Justification:	This is a measure of a few things. If the Service Desk has a good Known Error DB supplied by Problem Management the number of incidents resolved by the first line support will increase.
Audience:	Process Owner, IT Management, SLA Process Owner, Business Customer, Team Members, SIP Process Owner
Constraints:	If the Problem Management process succeeds in eliminating root causes, the part of Incidents resolvable by 1st line support will decrease, and consequently the number resolved by 1st line support may decrease.
Danger value:	<65
Target value:	85
Possible values:	0-100

Metric:	Average call time with no escalation {minutes}
Description:	This is a measure of effectiveness. This is balanced against Customer Satisfaction as calls must take long enough to satisfy the user requirement for resolution - but, with good tools and a good Known Error DB, this should be able to be reduced.
Specification:	How long do calls take if there is no escalation.
Justification:	Closing calls too quickly is not good for customer satisfaction. However the Service Desk does need to handle calls efficiently and this is a measure of that efficiency.

Audience:	Process Owner, IT Management, SLA Process Owner, Business Customer, Team Members, SIP Process Owner
Constraints:	None
Danger value:	>20
Target value:	10
Possible values:	999999

Metric:	**Percentage of incidents incorrectly assigned {%incidents}**
Description:	This is measured by checking the call history for re-assignment status. Specification: How many incidents are assigned to the wrong work-group.
Justification:	Re-assigning calls slows resolution and reduces the effectiveness of the teams. Good call handling scripts, training, tools and processes will reduce the incidence of this.
Audience:	Process Owner, IT Management, SLA Process Owner, Business Customer, Team Members, SIP Process Owner
Constraints:	None
Danger value:	30
Target value:	20
Possible values:	0-100

Metric:	**Percentage of incidents resolved within target time by priority {%incidents}**
Description:	When a call arrives at the Service Desk, it is allocated a target resolution time according to the SLA attached to the service and the priority of the call. This measures how often this target is achieved.
Specification:	Within target time by priority.
Justification:	This is a direct measure of how well the Service Desk is keeping to agreed SLAs.
Audience:	Process Owner, IT Management, SLA Process Owner, Business Customer, Team Members, SIP Process Owner
Constraints:	None
Danger value:	<90
Target value:	95
Possible values:	0-100

Metric:	**Average time for second level support to respond {minutes}**
Description:	This is the time between a call being assigned to second level support and the call being accepted. It is a measure of the effectiveness of second level support.
Specification:	Minutes
Justification:	Escalation to second level support is a threat to SLA times. The time between dispatch and acceptance of a call has a direct effect on how much longer the call is delayed. This metric ensures that this time is closely monitored and the acceptance process kept efficient.
Audience:	Process Owner, IT Management, SLA Process Owner, Business Customer, Team Members, SIP Process Owner

Constraints:	None
Danger value:	>10
Target value:	This is a matter of priorities. For example: 1 constitutes the highest priority and has 10 minutes as a maximum respond time, 2 is a medium priority and has 30 minutes as a maximum respond time, and 3 being has the lowest priority and it may take second level support 2 hours to respond.
Possible values:	999999

Metric:	**Average time to resolve incidents {minutes}**
Description:	This measures the major part of total call time - up to the resolution, when the user is satisfied with the resolution. Please note, it only measures the time an incident is in various states, and excludes the time 'waiting for user' and 'closed'.
Specification:	Minutes from call open to call resolved.
Justification:	This is a popular metric as it shows the overall effectiveness of the Incident Management process.
Audience:	Process Owner, IT Management, SLA Process Owner, Business Customer, Team Members, SIP Process Owner
Constraints:	This should not be measured as time from call open to call closed, but as time from call open to call resolved: the last step from call resolved until call closed is an administrative step which is not of interest to the customer. It can be used to take care of knowlegde base update, improve quality of registration, or other activities. The duration of this is of no interest to the customer and should therefore not be reported to the customer. The metric requires that the logging system discriminates between statusses 'call resolved' and 'call closed'.
Danger value:	>30
Target value:	20
Possible values:	999999

Metric:	**Percentage of incidents re-assigned {incidents}**
Description:	This measures incidents that are assigned to more than one second or third level resource (sometimes known as 'resolver groups').
Specification:	Incidents that have more than two assignments when closed. Normally incidents are closed with no assignment or with 'assigned to resource' then 'assigned to service desk', any further assignments will be counted here.
Justification:	Sometimes it is necessary to get assistance from other teams so reassigment is the proper course of action. However, more often, calls are assigned to the wrong team by mistake and then have to be re-assigned. This wastes time, decreases availability and indicates that the incident management process is not identifying the correct group. This metric enables the size of the problem to be seen and for steps to be put in place to correct mis-assignment through improved processes and improved information in the Known Error Database.

Audience:	Process Owner, IT Management, SLA Process Owner, Business Customer, Team Members, SIP Process Owner
Constraints:	None
Danger value:	>10
Target value:	10
Possible values:	0-100

Metric Objective: *To assist Problem Management in identifying trends in incidents. This also enables Problem Management to understand how well the Known Error Database and CMDB are performing.*

Metric:	**Percentage of incidents incorrectly categorized {%incidents}**
Description:	When calls are logged, they are assigned a category to assist in resolution and for later analysis. When calls are closed the real category is included. This measures how many calls have these two different.
Specification:	How many incidents have the wrong description or category when first categorized.
Justification:	Good categorization speeds resolution. How effective categorization is performed is a measure of the script used to get information from customers, the level of training given to the call centre staff and the effectiveness of the support environment - a good CMDB, for example, should help improve this.
Audience:	Process Owner, IT Management, SLA Process Owner, Business Customer, Team Members, SIP Process Owner
Constraints:	None
Danger value:	60
Target value:	40
Possible values:	0-100

Metric Objective: *To ensure that all incidents are detected and recorded.*

Metric:	**Percentage of calls 1st line support bypassed {%calls}**
Description:	How often do customers call second or third level support directly - measured by calls created in second and third line. It is important that all IT staff are comfortable about creating an incident if they are called in this way.
Specification:	Calls that do not come through the official channel.
Justification:	Direct calls to support staff have a number of disadvantages. The support staff lose time that should be devoted to other things. The Service Desk does not have a log of all incidents. This indicates that users do not trust the standard process.
Audience:	Process Owner, IT Management, SLA Process Owner, Business Customer, Team Members, SIP Process Owner
Constraints:	None

Danger value:	>10
Target value:	5
Possible values:	0-100

Metric Objective: *Effective IT Provision.*

Metric:	**Customer Satisfaction {satisfaction}**
Description:	This balances the other metrics. If the calls are closed too quickly or take too long then, whatever the internal metrics might say, Customer Satisfaction will start to suffer and that will be shown by this metric.
Specification:	Measured by asking the customer for a when a call is closed. Can be done every time or as a sample.
Justification:	This will always be one of the top three or four metrics for Incident Management. This is a very direct means of knowing how the general user community feels about the service being provided.
Audience:	Process Owner, IT Management, SLA Process Owner, Business Customer, Team Members, SIP Process Owner
Constraints:	Users shouldn't be bothered too much with this. Sampling is more likely to be accepted by the user than having to answer one or more questions after each call.
Danger value:	<3
Target value:	4
Possible values:	0-5

Metric:	**Percentage of calls that are service requests {%calls}**
Description:	The percentage of calls that are service requests, not incidents or other calls.
Specification:	Calls that are dealt with by the Service Desk as service requests.
Justification:	As the Service Desk becomes a trusted advisor to end users and as the number of incidents decreases, this metric should increase. A mark of a mature service desk is a high value for this metric. The target ought to start low as most people will see the Service Desk as renamed 'Help Desk' for technical problems only - over time, as perception catches up with the ambition for the Service Desk, the calls will increase, but, if a high proportion are service requests, then this is a good thing for service delivery to the business.
Audience:	Process Owner, IT Management, SLA Process Owner, Business Customer, Team Members, SIP Process Owner
Constraints:	To be useful, it is important that service requests are properly identified as such so that incidents can't be hidden as service requests.
Danger value:	5
Target value:	15
Possible values:	0-100

Metric:	**Percentage of incidents solved rightly the first time (First Time Right Resolution) {%incidents}**
Description:	The percentage of incidents that are resolved in the first attempt to resolve it. The incident doesn't need to be reopened nor do new incidents need to be created for the same event.
Specification:	The managers of the resolutions groups should use this metric to determine the effectiveness of their resolution group and to determine whether or not the experts in the resolution group have the right amount of knowledge and experience to resolve incidents.
Justification:	The more effective the resolution group, the lesser rework needs to be done and the higher customer satisfaction will be.
Audience:	Process Owner, IT Management, SLA Process Owner, Business Customer, Team Members, SIP Process Owner
Constraints:	Customers need to approve the resolution, it cannot be a technical resolution, the customer needs to accept it.
Danger value:	75 %
Target value:	90 %
Possible values:	1-100 %

Metric:	**Percentage of proactively solved incidents {%incidents}**
Description:	The percentage of resolved incident that were resolved before the customers reported an error (this has a strong linkage with the monitoring of systems and applications).
Specification:	Incidents resolved (because of events generated by monitoring tools) before customers experience problems are extremely important in the value added by service management processes.
Justification:	Proactively resolved incidents add value to the incident management process and have not disturbed business processes.
Audience:	Process Owner, IT Management, SLA Process Owner, Business Customer, Team Members, SIP Process Owner
Constraints:	Requires the existence of an active monitoring process.
Danger value:	0 %
Target value:	15 %
Possible values:	0-100 %

B   Service Desk metrics

> The **goals** of the **Service Desk** are:
>
> To provide a single point of contact for customers.
>
> To provide advice and guidance, and to facilitate the restoration of normal operational service with minimal business impact on the customer, within agreed service levels and business priorities.
>
> (OGC ITIL Best Practice for Service Support)

> **Mission Statement:**
> The Service Desk is the single point of contact for all incoming calls to the IT department, it will provide a customer focused interface between the users and IT to enable the efficient use of IT services, helping restore normal services as soon as possible as well as being proactive in advising users of potential service interruptions.

> **Process owner:** Service Desk Manager

> **Metric Objective:** To restore normal service operation as quickly as possible and minimize the adverse impact on business operations, thus ensuring the best possible levels of service quality.

Metric:	**Number of calls without escalation per agent {calls}**
Description:	What is the number of calls without escalation taken per person.
Specification:	The number of calls without escalation taken per service desk agent per day.
Justification:	This is the number of calls - with no escalation. That means that it is calls that have a duration less than the minimum escalation period for management escalation and are not escalated technically. That is it measures 'simple' or 'standard' calls that are dealt with entirely by the service desk agent with no technical or functional escalation. This is a simple, but important, measure of loading of each operator. If this is high it means either a problem with resources or an extremely efficient Service Desk - futher investigation or knowledge of the maturity of the organization will reveal which.
Audience:	Process Owner, IT Management, SLA Process Owner, Business Customer, Team Members, SIP Process Owner
Constraints:	None
Danger value:	40
Target value:	20
Possible values:	999999

Metric:	**Percentage of calls closed first time per agent {%calls}**
Description:	Simple calls with no escalation.
Specification:	The percentage of calls that are closed after the first call - with the answer given, a workaround or other reason to close.
Justification:	Since this is the ideal - for all calls to be dealt with at once at the first call - it is important to measure how close the Service Desk is to the ideal.
Audience:	Process Owner, IT Management, SLA Process Owner, Business Customer, Team Members, SIP Process Owner
Constraints:	None
Danger value:	40
Target value:	65
Possible values:	0-100

Metric:	**Number of calls that exceed SLA {calls}**
Description:	All CIs have to be linked to the appropriate service and this measures the service related to the call that exceeds its SLA first.
Specification:	The number of calls per day that exceed the SLA.
Justification:	This is a vital measure of the effectiveness of Service Desk output.
Audience:	Process Owner, IT Management, SLA Process Owner, Business Customer, Team Members, SIP Process Owner
Constraints:	None
Danger value:	8
Target value:	3
Possible values:	999999

Metric:	**Number of calls escalated to second Level Support {Calls}**
Description:	The number of calls per day that are escalated to second level support.
Specification:	Any calls that have a first escalation, per day.
Justification:	This is a measure of the usefulness of second level support - and also of how effective the Service Desk front-line support is. Ideally this will reduce over time as processes and the Known Error database improve. This metric partially overlaps the [% first call resolution] metric.
Audience:	Process Owner, IT Management, SLA Process Owner, Business Customer, Team Members, SIP Process Owner
Constraints:	None
Danger value:	10
Target value:	5
Possible values:	999999

Metric:	**Customer Satisfaction {satisfaction}**
Description:	Satisfaction is measured at the close of every Service Call or at a sample thereof.
Specification:	Include this as a high value until it is consistently good, then put it at lower priority. Measure it for each call, or over a fixed period of time. Justification: Ultimately, this is probably the top measure for the Service Desk.

Audience:	Process Owner, IT Management, SLA Process Owner, Business Customer, Team Members, SIP Process Owner
Constraints:	None
Danger value:	< 3
Target value:	4
Possible values:	0-5

Metric:	**Number of calls escalated to third Level Support {calls}**
Description:	Calls that need third level support to be solved.
Specification:	Calls per day, escalated from second to third level support.
Justification:	If this is too high it means improving the procedures and effectiveness of both first and second level support.
Audience:	Process Owner, IT Management, SLA Process Owner, Business Customer, Team Members, SIP Process Owner
Constraints:	None
Danger value:	6
Target value:	3
Possible values:	999999

Metric:	**Average time waiting for call to be answered {seconds}**
Description:	This measures the loading and resourcing of the Service Desk.
Specification:	The number of seconds that customers wait for their call to be answered.
Justification:	All sources of delay are a problem for meeting its objectives. This is an easily avoidable source with proper resourcing. It is also a source of quickly decreasing customer satisfaction.
Audience:	Process Owner, IT Management, SLA Process Owner, Business Customer, Team Members, SIP Process Owner
Constraints:	None
Danger value:	20
Target value:	10
Possible values:	999999

Metric:	**Average time spent trying to contact customers per call {minutes}**
Description:	Call waiting time.
Specification:	The number of minutes per call that the agent spends calling back a customer for more information or to give a solution.
Justification:	Of course users are busy and may be difficult to get back to. If this time is high then other methods (SMS, e-mail) might be used rather than telephone calls to reduce wasted time when Service Desk agents are tied up unproductively.
Audience:	Process Owner, IT Management, SLA Process Owner, Business Customer, Team Members, SIP Process Owner
Constraints:	None
Danger value:	10
Target value:	5
Possible values:	999999

Metric:	**Percentage of calls that come via the web {%calls}**
Description:	A measure of call source.
Specification:	The ideal is for most calls to be placed using the web interface.
Justification:	The easier and quicker it is to log a call accurately the better for overall solutions and solution times. This applies to other possible sources for calls like e-mail just as well. This also improves the effectiveness of the Service Desk as it can decide which users require follow-up calls and how these are to be managed.
Audience:	Process Owner, IT Management, SLA Process Owner, Business Customer, Team Members, SIP Process Owner
Constraints:	None
Danger value:	20
Target value:	60
Possible values:	0-100

Metric:	**Percentage of calls with wrong escalation {%calls}**
Description:	This is measured by a call being re-assigned with the reason being that it was wrongly assigned.
Specification:	The percentage of calls that are escalated to the wrong workgroup.
Justification:	The service desk aims to restore service as quickly as possible. Wrongful assingement is an avoidable delay that this measures.
Audience:	Process Owner, IT Management, SLA Process Owner, Business Customer, Team Members, SIP Process Owner
Constraints:	None
Danger value:	15
Target value:	5
Possible values:	0-100

Metric Objective: *Availability of the Service Desk to its customers.*

Metric:	**Percentage of calls dropped by users {%calls}**
Description:	When the telephone is the main input channel to the Service Desk, staffing has to be adequate to receive the calls, as well as staff should be ready to take incoming calls within the agreed ringing time. Otherwise users would not be able to report their issue.
Specification:	The number of calls where users abandon the call after the agreed waiting time or rings divided by the total number of calls that were recorded at the Automatic Call Distribution (ACD) system.
Justification:	This is an objective that contributes highly to User satisfaction. A high percentage would indicate low availability caused by inadequate staffing, long call handling times, inefficient processes.
Audience:	Process Owner, IT Management, SLA Process Owner, Business Customer, Team Members, SIP Process Owner

Constraints:	An ACD with the correct technology to record and report this is required. It is important to have an agreed number of rings and call workflow and not consider calls where user hangs before the agreed number of rings and workflow.
Danger value:	5%
Target value:	3%
Possible values:	1-100

Metric Objective: *Gauge the efficiency of the call handling process, to understand Service Desk workload.*

Metric:	**Percentage of calls converted to tickets {%calls}**
Description:	The Service Desk receives many calls, some of which may not be recorded in the ticketing system for various reasons (follow up). This metric gives an insight into how many calls were actually incidents or follow up calls, or calls to the wrong support (e.g., instead of Facilities users call IT Service desk), etc. A high number should trigger an investigation into what kind of calls are coming through and whether the Service Desk efficient in handling calls.
Specification:	Number of connected calls at the ACD to (divided by) number of tickets logged (with telephone as the source) per day.
Justification:	The Service Desk needs to have efficient call handling workflow in recording all calls into the ticketing system. Follow up calls need to be reduced by proactive mechanisms. Users need to be educated on the correct contact numbers. This metric gives an indication of all these which helps the Service Desk to be effective.
Audience:	Process Owner, IT Management, SLA Process Owner, Business Customer, Team Members, SIP Process Owner
Constraints:	This metric should be used where the telephone is the main input channel for incidents. The ACD needs to be able to produce call reports
Danger value:	=>1.1
Target value:	1
Possible values:	=>1

Metric Objective: *To analyze Service Desk workload and compute staffing requirements.*

Metric:	**Percentage of incidents from event management {%incidents}**
Description:	Enterprise management systems generate automated alerts that are integrated into the incident ticketing system to generate automated tickets which may also be routed to support teams automatically. This mechanism reduces the effort of logging calls by the Service Desk, and also helps proactive incident monitoring and management.
Specification:	Number of tickets generated by event management systems divided by total number of tickets for a period.

Justification:	The more the percentage, the less the effort of the Service Desk in logging calls and assigning them.
Audience:	Process Owner, IT Management, SLA Process Owner, Team Members, SIP Process Owner
Constraints:	The event management system's integration with the incident ticketing system should ensure avoidance of duplication of event-based tickets for the same event. Otherwise the metric would show a skewed number.
Danger value:	> 0
Target value:	0
Possible values:	0 - 100 %

Metric Objective: *to show the Service Desk has appropriate knowledge of the areas in which incidents occur and which resolution group is necessary to resolve it.*

Metric:	**Percentage of calls rightly assigned the first time (First time right assignment) {% incidents}**
Description:	The percentage of calls assigned by the service desk to the right resolutions groups shows the effectiveness of the service desk and makes sure the customer has confidence in calling the service desk.
Specification:	The amount of calls that are not rejected or immediately reassigned by the resolution groups.
Justification:	Correctly assigned calls make sure the resolution is effective and shows a professional process of handling. Furthermore it makes sure that calls are not assigned from one group to another. Audience Process Owner, IT Management, SLA Process Owner, Team Members, SIP Process Owner
Constraints:	The amount of knowledge on the service desk.
Danger value:	75 %
Target value:	90 %
Possible values:	0 - 100 %

C   Metrics for Configuration Management

> The **goals** of the **Configuration Management** process are:
>
> • Account for all the IT assets and configurations within the organization and its services.
> • Provide accurate information on configurations and their documentation to support all the other Service Management processes.
> • Provide a sound basis for Incident Management, Problem Management, Change Management and Release Management.
> • Verify the configuration records against the infrastructure and correct any exceptions.
>
> (OGC ITIL Best Practice for Service Support)

> **Mission Statement:** To identify, control and audit the information required to manage IT services by defining and maintaining a database of controlled items, their status, lifecycles and relationships and any information needed to manage the quality of IT services cost effectively.

> **Process owner:** Configuration Manager

> **Metric Objective:** To identify and manage the IT infrastructure information and relationships accurately and effectively according to business need and agreed policy standards.

Metric:	**Number of licenses not used {licenses}**
Description:	The CMDB has a record of all software licenses and where they are deployed, so a report of unused licenses can be produced.
Specification:	The Configuration Management process should have control of software licenses to minimize the cost of unused licenses.
Justification:	Some unused licenses are to be expected - they are there to provide for capacity needs over the next several weeks. A high level of unused licenses points to a Capacity Management problem - but that, in turn, points to a poor use of the CMDB by Capacity Management, which might be because of accuracy issues. This metric encourages Configuration Management to ensure that license information is accurate and that Configuration Management is using it to drive the number of unnecessary licenses to a minimum.
Audience:	Process Owner, IT Management, SLA Process Owner, Business Customer, Team Members, SIP Process Owner
Constraints:	None
Danger value:	80
Target value:	50
Possible values:	999999

Metric:	**Number of failed RFCs from bad CMDB data {RFCs}**
Description:	RFCs are based on CMDB information. If this is incorrect and they are eventually rejected by the Change Management process this must be recorded.
Specification:	To improve the quality of the CMDB, this metric must be low. Measuring it means that the Configuration Management team must work closely with the Change Manager to make sure that RFCs are consistent with the CMDB. This means that the quality will improve.
Justification:	Those creating RFCs must be able to rely on the CMDB to provide accurate data. RFCs ought not to be rejected because of bad CMDB information.
Audience:	Process Owner, IT Management, SLA Process Owner, Business Customer, Team Members, SIP Process Owner
Constraints:	None
Danger value:	20
Target value:	10
Possible values:	999999

Metric:	**Number of unauthorized configurations {configurations}**
Description:	Configurations in the CMDB that are not properly authorized.
Specification:	This is a matter of communication and management with the IT and user communities. This should eventually be very low indeed. Justification: All configurations must be properly authorized - the process must be clear and the CMDB must record these authorizations accurately. This measures that these processes are working.
Audience:	Process Owner, IT Management, SLA Process Owner, Business Customer, Team Members, SIP Process Owner
Constraints:	None
Danger value:	15
Target value:	5
Possible values:	999999

Metric:	**Number of incidents from failed changes caused by wrongly documented CIs {incidents}**
Description:	Changes are approved in terms of the CMDB which is taken as an authority. If a change fails because of wrong information about a component then it is the responsibility of Configuration Management.
Specification:	This may be high to begin with - this metric should help bring it down.
Justification:	CI information in the CMDB must be correct - so changes will be correct, and so incidents will not arise from them.
Audience:	Process Owner, IT Management, SLA Process Owner, Team Members, SIP Process Owner
Constraints:	The closing disposition of incidents must be able to record incidents that were a result of a change and that the change failed because of poor CMDB accuracy.

Danger value:	6
Target value:	0
Possible values:	999999

Metric:	**Number of breached SLA because of CMDB errors {SLAs}**
Description:	First priority to begin with to make sure that enough accuracy is in the CMDB to prevent breeching SLA. Eventually it should be accepted that this is always 0 - then, when it has been 0 for some months, another metric can be substituted.
Specification:	This should never happen. Once the CMDB is in place and Configuration Management controls are working well with good Change Management, outages ought not to occur because of problems with the CMDB. This is measured by reference to the closing status of calls.
Justification:	Inaccuracies or missing elements in the CMDB can lead to poor problem solving and even poor Incident Management - this is measured by this metric. As Configuration Management improves the reduction of this towards nil this metric can be seen as a good measure of its maturity.
Audience:	Process Owner, IT Management, SLA Process Owner, Business Customer, Team Members, SIP Process Owner
Constraints:	None
Danger value:	2
Target value:	0
Possible values:	999999

Metric Objective: *To ensure CMDB provides accurate information to other processes.*

Metric:	**Number of RFCs without corresponding CI updating {RFCs}**
Description:	Every time a CI undergoes a change, there has to be a corresponding authorized RFC and a subsequent updating of the CMDB to reflect the change completion. During an audit, the RFC is compared with the configuration information in the CMDB. They should match. This could also be a percentage of the total number of RFCs raised for a period.
Specification:	During an audit, the number of RFCs for which the CMDB does not show corresponding configuration status.
Justification:	This ensures accurate and authorized information in the CMDB by process adherence.
Audience:	Process Owner, IT Management, SLA Process Owner, Team Members, SIP Process Owner
Constraints:	None
Danger value:	=> 5, at any point of time
Target value:	None
Possible values:	99999

Metric:	**Percentage of inaccurate CIs {%CIs}**
Description:	All corrections to CIs to improve accuracy must be counted to contribute to this metric.
Specification:	The quality of data input is important - some of the data comes from other tools and organizations so it might take time before this can be reduced to a consistently low level. This is measured as inaccurate CIs as a percentage of total CIs - since we know how many CIs exist in the CMDB at any time, we can measure this as a percentage.
Justification:	Configuration Management processes are designed to ensure the accuracy of CI information. If this metric is not reducing over time then the SIP ought to see where effectiveness can be improved.
Audience:	Process Owner, IT Management, SLA Process Owner, Team Members, SIP Process Owner
Constraints:	None
Danger value:	80
Target value:	40
Possible values:	0-100

Metric Objective: To provide effective Service Management processes.

Metric:	**Customer Satisfaction {satisfaction}**
Description:	Customer Satisfaction measured by reference to the Process Relationship diagram.
Specification:	Customer Satisfaction measured by reference to the Process Relationship diagram.
Justification:	A test of the effectiveness of this process.
Audience:	Process Owner, IT Management, SLA Process Owner, Business Customer, Team Members, SIP Process Owner
Constraints:	None
Danger value:	< 3
Target value:	4
Possible values:	0-5

D   Metrics for Change Management

The **goal** of the **Change Management** process is to ensure that standardized methods and procedures are used for efficient and prompt handling of all changes, in order to minimize the impact of change-related incidents upon service quality, and consequently to improve the day-to-day operation of the organization. (OGC ITIL Best Practice for Service Support)

Mission Statement: To manage all changes that could impact on IT's ability to deliver services through a formal, centralized process of approval, scheduling and control to ensure that the IT infrastructure stays aligned to business requirements with a minimum of risk.

Process owner: Change Manager

Metric Objective: Change Management to be an effective process for implementing changes required by the organization.

Metric:	**Percentage of failed changes {%changes}**
Description:	RFCs that have been approved, but then fail to be implemented.
Specification:	Changes that have failed to complete. Justification: The Change Management process ought to recognize risk in RFCs and not approve those that will not complete properly.
Audience:	Process Owner, IT Management, SLA Process Owner, Business Customer, Team Members, SIP Process Owner
Constraints:	None
Danger value:	10
Target value:	5
Possible values:	0-100

Metric:	**Percentage of rejected RFCs {%RFCs}**
Description:	Change proposals are screened (mainly by the Service Desk). Once a change has been accepted and developed to the level of having an RFC, there ought to be a fair chance of it succeeding. This measures how well the screening process is working.
Specification:	This is kept low by good communication.
Justification:	Poor requests for change ought to be screened early. Good processes ought to be in place to ensure that RFCs are produced to a standard of detail to prevent their being rejected.
Audience:	Process Owner, IT Management, SLA Process Owner, Business Customer, Team Members, SIP Process Owner
Constraints:	None
Danger value:	20
Target value:	10
Possible values:	0-100

Metric:	**Number of unauthorized changes {changes}**
Description:	Any change to the infrastructure that is detected for which there is not a standard change or an approved RFC.
Specification:	This is kept low by good communication.
Justification:	All changes must be under change control.
Audience:	Process Owner, IT Management, SLA Process Owner, Business Customer, Team Members, SIP Process Owner
Constraints:	None
Danger value:	30
Target value:	15
Possible values:	999999

Metric:	**Change backlog {changes}**
Description:	This measures two things. One is the number of approved changes that have not been actioned within target time, the other is the number of RFCs that have not been approved or rejected.
Specification:	If this is big, the organization is not coping. Maybe there is too much change or not enough people working on changes.
Justification:	Changes must be executed as close to the target time as possible. If RFCs are queued and not actioned, there is a risk to the business that a change that will prevent business disruption is not acted upon in time.
Audience: Process	Owner, IT Management, SLA Process Owner, Business Customer, Team Members, SIP Process Owner
Constraints:	None
Danger value:	15
Target value:	5
Possible values:	999999

Metric:	**Outages during changes {incidents}**
Description:	Any service outages will be measured by incidents. If a change occurs out of service hours then there can, by definition, be no service outage.
Specification:	In an ideal world there will never be any unplanned outages during changes. Justification: If a change is seen to be failing then it must be backed out before it impacts services. The back-out plan ought to have been tested so that a back-out does not result in any service outages.
Audience:	Process Owner, IT Management, SLA Process Owner, Business Customer, Team Members, SIP Process Owner
Constraints:	None
Danger value:	6
Target value:	0
Possible values:	999999

Metric:	**Number of failed changes with no back-out plan {changes}**
Description:	Any change that has the status failed and does not have a back-out plan counts.
Specification:	All changes should have a back out plan - this should always be checked.
Justification:	No change should be without a properly tested back-out plan. If a change fails and lacks a plan then, at least, poor risk analysis has been performed.
Audience:	Process Owner, IT Management, SLA Process Owner, Business Customer, Team Members, SIP Process Owner
Constraints:	None
Danger value:	2
Target value:	0
Possible values:	999999

Metric:	**Percentage of changes on time {%changes}**
Description:	All changes have a completion time. If they are still open after this time they count towards this metric.
Specification:	Delays can be caused by good reasons - if Percentage of Failed Changes is low then a high value here might be OK, so it should be a lower priority.
Justification:	If changes are consistently late then it shows poor change control and an increased risk of business disruption.
Audience:	Process Owner, IT Management, SLA Process Owner, Business Customer, Team Members, SIP Process Owner
Constraints:	None
Danger value:	90
Target value:	95
Possible values:	0-100

Metric:	**Percentage of changes causing incidents {%changes}**
Description:	Any incident that is found, on closing, to have been caused by a change is counted towards this metric.
Specification:	If there is a danger of changes causing incidents they should be done out of SLA hours during planned downtime. If changes cause incidents, it is probably a result of bad planning or testing.
Justification:	Changes should never cause business disruption.
Audience:	Process Owner, IT Management, SLA Process Owner, Business Customer, Team Members, SIP Process Owner
Constraints:	None
Danger value:	10
Target value:	5
Possible values:	0-100

Metric:	**Number of CAB items not actioned on time {actions}**
Description:	Any documented action item for the CAB will have a date for the action to take place. If this date is past without the action it counts towards this metric.
Specification:	All CAB items should be acted on - this metric should be unnecessary, but, if it does have a high value then the organization might be under too much stress. Compare this with the backlog metric.
Justification:	The CAB must be responsive. Otherwise the Change Manager cannot make effective decisions.
Audience:	Process Owner, IT Management, SLA Process Owner, Team Members, SIP Process Owner
Constraints:	CAB documents and action items must be under proper document control.
Danger value:	3
Target value:	0
Possible values:	999999

Metric:	**Number of Emergency Changes {Changes}**
Description:	All changes that go through the Emergency Change process.
Specification:	The Change process is designed to deal with all that is required effectively so as to reduce the risk inherent in any change. The Emergency Change process allows for some of the safeguards (testing in particular) to be reduced or circumvented. This increased risk, though occasionally inevitable, must be kept to a reasonable minimum. This metric shows any trend to overuse the process allowing corrective action to be taken.
Justification:	There will always be the occasional need for Emergency Changes, however it is vital that they never become a normal way of operating. This metric keeps track of how often the exception process is used.
Audience:	Process Owner, IT Management, SLA Process Owner, Business Customer, Team Members, SIP Process Owner
Constraints:	None
Danger value:	3
Target value:	3
Possible values:	999999

Metric:	**Number of Changes that do not deliver expected results {Changes}**
Description:	Changes that don't produce the results planned in the RFC.
Specification:	Changes are defined in the RFC which includes the expected outcome. When the change is complete, a change review occurs which checks that the change went smoothly and that the outcome was as expected. If the status after this shows that the change did not have the expected outcome then it will count towards this metric.
Justification:	Planning and testing are expected to ensure that RFCs result in effective changes that are not disruptive and produce the desired result. The change review checks to see if this has happened. This metric closes the loop and shows if the end-to-end change process is delivering the expected improvements.

Audience:	Process Owner, IT Management, SLA Process Owner, Business Customer, Team Members, SIP Process Owner
Constraints:	Clear and measurable target values are needed to be able to judge whether a change meets expectations.
Danger value:	3
Target value:	3
Possible values:	999999

Metric Objective: *High quality IT Service Management processes.*

Metric:	**Customer Satisfaction {satisfaction}**
Description:	Internal satisfaction with the Change Management process measured for every RFC.
Specification:	Measured in relation to the Process Relationship diagram.
Justification:	This is a sound measure of the quality of output.
Audience:	Process Owner, IT Management, SLA Process Owner, Business Customer, Team Members, SIP Process Owner
Constraints:	None
Danger value:	< 3
Target value:	4
Possible values:	0-5

E   Metrics for Release Management

The **goals** of **Release Management** are:
- To plan and oversee the successful rollout of software and related hardware.
- To design and implement efficient procedure for the distribution and installation of changes to IT systems.
- To ensure that hardware and software being changed is traceable, secure and that only correct, authorized and tested versions are installed.
- To communicate and manage expectations of the customer during the planning and rollout of new releases.
- To agree the exact content and rollout plan for the release, through liaison with Change Management.
- To implement new software releases or hardware into the operational environment using the controlling processes of Configuration Management and Change Management. A release should be under Change Management and may consist of any combination of hardware, software, firmware and document CIs.
- To ensure that master copies of all software are secured in the Definitive Software Library (DSL) and that the Configuration Management Database (CMDB) is updated.
- To ensure that all hardware being rolled out or changed is secure and traceable, using the services of Configuration Management.

(OGC ITIL Best Practice for Service Support)

Mission Statement: To take a holistic view of a change to an IT service and ensure that all aspects of a release, both technical and non-technical, are considered together.

Process owner: Release Manager

Metric Objective: To keep an accurate record of all definitive software revisions in the DSL.

Metric:	Installed software packages not in DSL {packages}
Description:	Any software discovered on any equipment can, as part of the standard verification process, be checked against the DSL to see that it is authorized and of the correct revision.
Specification:	The amount of software that is installed, but not taken from the Definitive Software Library (DSL). A regular software audit (maybe carried out by a monitoring tool) may be needed to identify this.
Justification:	It is both a high security risk and an indication of poor Release Management and control for any software in the IT infrastructure not to be properly recorded in the DSL.
Audience:	Process Owner, IT Management, SLA Process Owner, Business Customer, Team Members, SIP Process Owner

Constraints:	None
Danger value:	50
Target value:	25
Possible values:	999999

Metric Objective: *To control the release of software into the infrastructure to ensure a minimum of disruption.*

Metric:	**Number of urgent releases {releases}**
Description:	Urgent releases follow the urgent release process - when this is invoked it can be recorded for use in this metric.
Specification:	Ideally all releases will be planned in advanced and installed to plan - urgent releases should be reduced over time.
Justification:	Urgent releases pose a high risk of error and hence service disruption to the business. There are times when they are justified, but they ought to be very rare. If this metric shows anything more than a handful a month it is cause for great concern.
Audience:	Process Owner, IT Management, SLA Process Owner, Business Customer, Team Members, SIP Process Owner
Constraints:	None
Danger value:	5
Target value:	0
Possible values:	999999

Metric Objective: *To manage releases effectively with a minimum of disruption to the business.*

Metric:	**Number of incidents caused by release {incidents}**
Description:	The closing disposition of all incident records should include Release Management as a potential cause. When this is recorded it will contribute to this metric.
Specification:	Well tested and planned releases should not give rise to incidents.
Justification:	Releases must be built and tested with proper back-out plans so that incidents are not caused as a result of them.
Audience:	Process Owner, IT Management, SLA Process Owner, Business Customer, Team Members, SIP Process Owner
Constraints:	None
Danger value:	50
Target value:	5
Possible values:	999999

Metric:	**Percentage of releases on time {%releases}**
Description:	Release Management includes planned dates for all parts of all releases in the CMDB. If any of these change, they will add to this metric.
Specification:	As planning improves all releases should be on time.
Justification:	There are good reasons to change release dates. However, good consultation with all stakeholders in advance should make changes unusual.
Audience:	Process Owner, IT Management, SLA Process Owner, Business Customer, Team Members, SIP Process Owner
Constraints:	None
Danger value:	90
Target value:	95
Possible values:	0-100

Metric:	**Number of untested releases {releases}**
Description:	All releases ought to have a test carried out and signed off by a person independent of the person who built the release. If this is missing at the time of the release then it will count as part of this metric.
Specification:	This is an important metric, if untested releases are used there is a danger of incidents and downtime being caused.
Justification:	Even emergency releases ought to be tested. Any untested release poses a very high risk to business continuity.
Audience:	Process Owner, IT Management, SLA Process Owner, Business Customer, Team Members, SIP Process Owner
Constraints:	None
Danger value:	0
Target value:	0
Possible values:	999999

Metric:	**Average cost of release {hours}**
Description:	Actual costs in man-hours are the simple measure.
Specification:	(In man-hours) The target and limits are simply guesses here. It will be necessary to measure this to determine reasonable values. Over time, the goal is to reduce the cost per release. In a more sophisticated environment, the difference between forecast hours (in the release plan) and actual hours might be substituted.
Justification:	Releases must be designed to be cost effective.
Audience:	Process Owner, IT Management, SLA Process Owner, Business Customer, Team Members, SIP Process Owner
Constraints:	Financial Management must be fairly effective for this to be properly measured. Good Project Management processes ought to be able to give a good estimate though.

Danger value:	500
Target value:	300
Possible values:	999999

Metric:	**Number of unused software licenses {licenses}**
Description:	Software licenses that are not installed and not justified by Capacity Management.
Specification:	Software licenses should only be paid for on CIs that are authorized to have software installed from the DSL. All other licenses should be terminated.
Justification:	If the CMDB is working properly, it ought to be possible to identify these easily. Working closely with Capacity Management to ensure that licenses that are genuinely required in the next few weeks or months are retained.
Audience:	Process Owner, IT Management, SLA Process Owner, Business Customer, Team Members, SIP Process Owner
Constraints:	None
Danger value:	200
Target value:	100
Possible values:	999999

Metric:	**Percentage of accuracy of release estimates {%time}**
Description:	Simply put this is the absolute difference in planned time from actual time.
Specification:	This is a composite metric, made up of the estimated time it would take to make the release, the man hours used for the release, the number of CIs affected by the release. The estimate must be preserved when the release planning is complete, then tested when the release has been deployed, this percentage is the difference between the actual and planned expressed as a percentage of the planned time.
Justification:	Forecast accuracy allows sound business decisions to be made. Improvement in forecasting in small releases ought also to increase the confidence in forecasts for large critically important releases.
Audience:	Process Owner, IT Management, SLA Process Owner, Business Customer, Team Members, SIP Process Owner
Constraints:	Good Project or Financial Management processes will be required to get the figures accurate.
Danger value:	60
Target value:	80
Possible values:	0-100 %

Metric Objective: *To provide effective Service Management processes.*

Metric: **Customer Satisfaction {satisfaction}**

Description: Include this as a high value until it is consistently good, then put it at lower priority.

Specification: As shown by the Process Relationship Diagram. In this case, though, end user satisfaction reports with particular roll-outs must also be included where they are available.

Justification: Release Management has a major impact on end users and it is important that they have had proper communication, awareness and training. Their level of satisfaction with the process will reflect how well this has been provided.

Audience: Process Owner, IT Management, SLA Process Owner, Business Customer, Team Members, SIP Process Owner

Constraints: None

Danger value: < 3

Target value: 4

Possible values: 0-5

E.1   Application Support metrics

Metric: **Number of bugs investigated {bugs}**

Description: This is a measure of the maintainability of the code. Ideally there will be more enhancements than bug fixes.

Specification: The list of bugs allocated and signed off as completed supplies the measure.

Justification: There are more detailed measures. This lacks the discrimination between easy and difficult problems to solve.

Audience: Process Owner, IT Management, SLA Process Owner, Business Customer, Team Members, SIP Process Owner

Constraints: This metric is influenced by the quality of the code itself, in terms of the number of errors that could be corrected. A measured value that is higher than the Target Value could then indicate that more bugs were attacked than expected, which is a good thing if you look at the process and the maintainability of the code - but it's not so good if you would use it as a measure of the quality of the code.

Danger value: 2

Target value: 4

Possible values: 999999

Metric: **Number of optimizations {optimizations}**

Description: Optimizations logged and approved.

Specification: This covers improvements to the code that are not approved enhancements or bug fixes. These improvements must be managed, as one of the objectives of Capacity Management is to improve the performance of applications. This is a measure of that activity.

Justification:	It is important that applications use resources effectively. New applications ought to be designed with performance as an objective, but existing ones can be improved.
Audience:	Process Owner, IT Management, SLA Process Owner, Business Customer, Team Members, SIP Process Owner
Constraints:	This metric is influenced by the quality of the code itself, in terms of the number of potential improvements that could be implemented. A measured value that is higher than the Target Value could then indicate that more potential improvements were attacked than expected, which is a good thing if you look at the process and the maintainability of the code - but it's not so good if you would use it as a measure of the quality of the code.
Danger value:	10
Target value:	20
Possible values:	999999

Metric:	**Number of applications/revisions released to production {builds}**
Description:	Accepted releases.
Specification:	As measured by Release Management in the DSL.
Justification:	This is a measure of genuine delivered productivity - which not necessarily relates to the quality of the application.
Audience:	Process Owner, IT Management, SLA Process Owner, Business Customer, Team Members, SIP Process Owner
Constraints:	Needs to take conditions into account: if customers do not require enhancements and the code is fault-free, there will simply be very few releases.
Danger value:	2
Target value:	4
Possible values:	999999

Metric:	**Number of end-user training sessions {training sessions}**
Description:	End-user training for new releases or new hires.
Specification:	This measures the on-going training of the user base as well as one-off training for new releases. This is an important measure of communication between Application Support and users. All too often training is neglected as it is not a measure of the success of Application Support. This is intended to address that problem.
Justification:	Though the actual delivery of training is the responsibility of Release Management, the writing of training materials and the monitoring of the quality of the courses is a responsibility of Application Support.
Audience:	Process Owner, IT Management, SLA Process Owner, Business Customer, Team Members, SIP Process Owner
Constraints:	Depending on user community stability
Danger value:	5
Target value:	10
Possible values:	99999

Metric:	**Number of defects detected from log files {bugs}**
Description:	This is simply the number of new bugs found by Application Support themselves. Other sources of information as well as log files will supply this. It is a measure of how many defects are listed as being discovered by Application Support.
Specification:	It is normal to fix bugs that have been found by users. It is, of course, better to fix them before they are found by users so that no service disruption occurs. This is a measure of the problem solving work to uncover bugs before they appear. It could be measured as an absolute value as well as per person working in Application Support.
Justification:	Measures that can improve the quality of the service to the business are important. A high level of problems discovered and fixed before they become incidents is usually invisible. It ought to be visible and encouraged.
Audience:	Process Owner, IT Management, SLA Process Owner, Business Customer, Team Members, SIP Process Owner
Constraints:	Depending on the quality of the code itself.
Danger value:	2
Target value:	4
Possible values:	999999

Metric:	**Number of production fixes {fixes}**
Description:	Production fixes.
Specification:	These include all fixes logged by Release Management. It could be measured as an absolute value as well as per person working in Application Support.
Justification:	These will include non-coding fixes, such as configuration fixes that are the direct responsibility of Application Support as well as code fixes that it is responsible for testing.
Audience:	Process Owner, IT Management, SLA Process Owner, Team Members, SIP Process Owner
Constraints:	Depending on the quality of the code itself.
Danger value:	3
Target value:	5
Possible values:	999999

Metric:	**Number of fixes returned to development {fixes}**
Description:	Fixes that did not work.
Specification:	Fixes rejected by Release Management or rolled-back in production deployment. It could be measured as an absolute value as well as per person working in Application Support.
Justification:	This is an indication of poor testing.
Audience:	Process Owner, IT Management, SLA Process Owner, Team Members, SIP Process Owner

Constraints:	Depending on the quality of the code itself.
Danger value:	1
Target value:	2
Possible values: 9	99999

E.2 Application Development metrics

Metric:	**Number of defects found during development or testing {defects}**
Description:	Defects logged against in-house software.
Specification:	These are found during development or testing but not live deployment. It could be measured as an absolute value as well as per person working in Application Support.
Justification:	These are a measure of the reliability of code produced.
Audience:	Process Owner, IT Management, SLA Process Owner, Team Members, SIP Process Owner
Constraints:	Depending on the quality of the code itself.
Danger value:	10
Target value:	20
Possible values:	999999

Metric:	**Number of defects fixed during testing {defects}**
Description:	Measured by defects logged as fixed and tested.
Specification:	These are defects discovered during testing. It could be measured as an absolute value as well as per person working in Application Support.
Justification:	A measure of productivity.
Audience:	Process Owner, IT Management, SLA Process Owner, Team Members, SIP Process Owner
Constraints:	Depending on the quality of the code itself.
Danger value:	20
Target value:	25
Possible values:	999999

Metric:	**Number of reported bugs fixed {bugs}**
Description:	Service disrupting software defects.
Specification:	Bugs determined to be the underlying problem from incidents logged at the Service Desk. It could be measured as an absolute value as well as per person working in Application Support.
Justification:	Unlike software defects detected through testing, these are known to have caused incidents, so it is important that they are fixed.
Audience:	Process Owner, IT Management, SLA Process Owner, Team Members, SIP Process Owner
Constraints:	Depending on the quality of the code itself.
Danger value:	5
Target value:	10
Possible values:	999999

Metric:	**Number of applications/revisions accepted as deployed {builds}**
Description:	Working releases.
Specification:	From Release Management, the number of releases deployed successfully.
Justification:	This is a measure of overall productivity and successful deployment.
Audience:	Process Owner, IT Management, SLA Process Owner, Team Members, SIP Process Owner
Constraints:	None
Danger value:	1
Target value:	3
Possible values:	999999

Metric:	**Number of applications/revisions rejected by Application Support {builds}**
Description:	Defective builds.
Specification:	Builds submitted for release but rejected by Application Support in Release Management.
Justification:	This is a measure of the quality of builds. Over time this should be a very low figure as testing improves.
Audience:	Process Owner, IT Management, SLA Process Owner, Team Members, SIP Process Owner
Constraints:	None
Danger value:	3
Target value:	1
Possible values:	999999

Metric:	**Number of application designs signed off by business {designs}**
Description:	Approved designs.
Specification:	Designs accepted by the Business.
Justification:	This ensures that the design process is transparent and approved by the business.
Audience:	Process Owner, IT Management, SLA Process Owner, Business Customer, Team Members, SIP Process Owner
Constraints:	Designs must be under document control. Depending upon Business activity.
Danger value:	10
Target value:	2
Possible values:	999999

Metric:	**Number of successful application builds {builds}**
Description:	These are measured by builds submitted to the DSL, which contains interim non-production builds as well as production builds.
Specification:	Builds built and tested in development.
Justification:	This is a measure of internal productivity. Internal builds that are tested and found acceptable may go on to alpha or beta testing, or even production.

Audience:	Process Owner, IT Management, SLA Process Owner, Team Members, SIP Process Owner
Constraints:	Depending upon Business activity.
Danger value:	6
Target value:	2
Possible values:	999999

Metric:	**Number of days deployment slipped {days}**
Description:	The time is measured from the agreed delivery date of tested code to the DSL.
Specification:	This is for all applications/versions.
Justification:	A measure of how effective Application Development is at working to schedules.
Audience:	Process Owner, IT Management, SLA Process Owner, Team Members, SIP Process Owner
Constraints:	None
Danger value:	10
Target value:	5
Possible values:	999999

F   Metrics for Operations Management/ICT Infrastructure Management

*The **goals** of **ICT Infrastructure Management** are:*

Design and Planning:
- *Meet the existing ICT requirements of the business.*
- *Innovate more effective ICT and business solutions.*
- *Be easily developed and enhanced to meet the future business needs of the organization, within appropriate time-scales and costs.*
- *Develop the soft skills within ICT by moving strategy into everyday operational tasks.*
- *Make effective and efficient use of all ICT resources and secure ICT environments.*
- *Contribute to the improvement of the overall quality of ICT service within the imposed cost constraints.*
- *Reduce, minimize or constrain long-term costs.*

Deployment:
- *Meet the existing needs of the business.*
- *Provide a suitable and stable ICT environment that can evolve or adapt to meet the future needs of the business.*
- *Contribute to overall improvements in the quality of ICT services.*

Operations:
- *To operate, manage and maintain an end-to-end ICT infrastructure that facilitates the delivery of the ICT services to the business, and that meets all its agreed requirements and targets.*
- *To ensure that the ICT infrastructure is reliable, robust, secure, consistent and facilitates the efficient and effective business processes of the organization.*

Technical Support:
The primary goal of Technical Support is to ensure that the business has highly available, cost-effective ICT services that underpin business objectives. To achieve this goal, Technical Support provides the necessary resources, skills and competencies to underpin the other ICTIM processes. Technical Support therefore needs to become a centre of technical excellence and assist Operations and Deployment in the provision of end-to-end services.

(OGC ITIL Best Practice for ICT Infrastructure Management)

> **Mission Statement:** *To manage and deliver high quality ICT services in line with business requirements in the areas of Design and Planning, Deployment, Operations and Technical Support.*

> **Process owner:** *ICT Infrastructure Manager*

> **Metric Objective:** *To manage and deliver high quality ICT services in line with business requirements in the areas of Design and Planning, Deployment, Operations and Technical Support.*

Metric:	**Number of plans signed off by the business {plans}**
Description:	Agreed plans.
Specification:	Design & Planning. The strategic plan will contain sub-plans to be deployed during the life of the strategy. These plans must each be completed in detail and signed off by the business owners using the criteria from the strategy.
Justification:	Plans must be properly managed and signed off. This is a measure of the productivity of this process.
Audience:	Process Owner, IT Management, SLA Process Owner, Business Customer, Team Members, SIP Process Owner
Constraints:	None
Danger value:	5
Target value:	2
Possible values:	999999

Metric:	**Number of plans not ready for sign-off {plans}**
Description:	Plans in the pipeline.
Specification:	Design & Planning. This is a measure of the number of plans in the strategic document that are due this month but not ready for sign off.
Justification:	This is a measure of future productivity. It might also, if large, be an indication of a shortage of resources.
Audience:	Process Owner, IT Management, SLA Process Owner, Team Members, SIP Process Owner
Constraints:	None
Danger value:	5
Target value:	2
Possible values:	999999

Metric:	**Delay from deployment plan {time}**
Description:	Plans delayed. Delay in actual deployment dates relative to planned deployment dates. Measured from the Forward Schedule of Changes.
Specification:	Deployment. The deployment plan will have milestones, this is the measure of delay against these milestones, in days.
Justification:	This is a measure of effectiveness. A high figure probably indicates a problem with resources or a problem with planning deployment.

Audience:	Process Owner, IT Management, SLA Process Owner, Business Customer, Team Members, SIP Process Owner
Constraints:	None
Danger value:	7
Target value:	2
Possible values:	999999

Metric:	**Number of defects during deployment {events/incidents}**
Description:	Any difficulties found during deployments.
Specification:	Deployment. The defects are events or incidents that occur as a result of the deployment. Possible overlap with Change Management metric "Percentage of changes causing incidents".
Justification:	Deployment ought to be planned not to disrupt services.
Audience:	Process Owner, IT Management, SLA Process Owner, Business Customer, Team Members, SIP Process Owner
Constraints:	None
Danger value:	5
Target value:	2
Possible values:	999999

Metric:	**Number of serious or critical events per Managed Object (MO) {events}**
Description:	Measured from the infrastructure monitoring tool this measures stability.
Specification:	Operations. The number of serious or critical events per Managed Object.
Justification:	Operations task is to maintain a stable infrastructure. This measures how effective this has been.
Audience:	Process Owner, IT Management, SLA Process Owner, Business Customer, Team Members, SIP Process Owner
Constraints:	None
Danger value:	0.03
Target value:	0.01
Possible values:	999999

Metric:	**Number of security events {events}**
Description:	Measured from the infrastructure monitoring tool.
Specification:	Operations. The management of firewalls and virus removal programs should keep these to a minimum. This count normally is per day since most viruses appear on a daily base and require immediate response.
Justification:	Though the concern of Security and Availability Management, the day-today operation of firewalls and other security devices is an operational responsibility. This metric relates to the number of security incidents: the former should always be lower. If both metrics are equal it would indicate poor responsiveness in Infrastructure Management.
Audience:	Process Owner, IT Management, SLA Process Owner, Business Customer, Team Members, SIP Process Owner

Constraints:	None
Danger value:	250
Target value:	150
Possible values:	999999

Metric:	**Number of job/script/backup failures {events}**
Description:	Scripting, hardware or process errors in Operations.
Specification:	Operations. The number of job/script/backup failures.
Justification:	All scripts and jobs are part of the DSL, failures will require changes to these or to operational procedures. It is important that these are kept to a minimum as they can be service affecting.
Audience:	Process Owner, IT Management, SLA Process Owner, Business Customer, Team Members, SIP Process Owner
Constraints:	None
Danger value:	20
Target value:	5
Possible values:	999999

Metric:	**Number of incidents as a result of operational changes {incidents}**
Description:	Serious operational incidents.
Specification:	Measured by the closing disposition on incidents that list operations as a cause. Overlap with Change Management metric "Percentage of changes causing incidents".
Justification:	Operational changes should take place out of service hours, so this should be very low. It is important to measure to make sure that it remains low.
Audience:	Process Owner, IT Management, SLA Process Owner, Business Customer, Team Members, SIP Process Owner
Constraints:	None
Danger value:	10
Target value:	5
Possible values:	999999

Metric Objective: *Effective IT provision.*	

Metric:	**Customer Satisfaction {satisfaction}**
Description:	Customer Satisfaction
Specification:	Customer Satisfaction measured as defined in the Process Relationship diagram.
Justification:	This is a measure of the effectiveness of IT provision.
Audience:	Process Owner, IT Management, SLA Process Owner, Business Customer, Team Members, SIP Process Owner
Constraints:	None
Danger value:	< 3
Target value:	4
Possible values:	0-5

G Metrics for Service Level Management

> The **goal** of **Service Level Management** (SLM) is to maintain and improve IT service quality, through a constant cycle of agreeing, monitoring and reporting upon IT service achievements and instigation of actions to eradicate poor service, in line with business or cost justification. Through these methods, a better relationship between IT and its customers can be developed.
>
> (OGC ITIL Best Practice for Service Delivery)

> **Mission Statement:** To manage the process of negotiating, defining and managing the level of IT services for the cost effective delivery of services that support the business goals of the organization.

> **Process owner:** Service Level Manager

> **Metric Objective:** IT Service Management provides effective services to levels agreed to with the business.

Metric:	**Number of SLA targets missed {incidents}**
Description:	This should be kept low. If this turns out to be high, then there must be an exceptional situation or SLAs must be re-negotiated.
Specification:	Any incident, Service Call, or agreed performance target outside the SLA is covered.
Justification:	This is a measure of times when the service levels have not been met and it is important for IT to have explanations for these for the business as well as agreed actions to resolve them. This metric ensures that this is kept as an important focus.
Audience:	Process Owner, IT Management, SLA Process Owner, Business Customer, Team Members, SIP Process Owner
Constraints:	None
Danger value:	25
Target value:	10
Possible values:	999999

Metric:	**Number of SLA targets threatened {SLAs}**
Description:	This is a measure of how close IT comes to breaching SLAs.
Specification:	This includes all escalations that occur because an SLA target will be breached within thirty minutes or less. This can be refined to be a percentage of the escalation time, where targets will be breached within eighty per cent of the escalation time, for example.

Justification:	Though the business is properly concerned only with actual breaches of agreed SLAs, the process owner and IT must be concerned with any incidents that seriously threaten the SLA thresholds.
Audience:	Process Owner, IT Management, SLA Process Owner, Business Customer, Team Members, SIP Process Owner
Constraints:	None
Danger value:	25
Target value:	10
Possible values:	999999

Metric:	**Percentage of SLAs that require changes {%SLAs}**
Description:	This measures unplanned changes to SLA outside of review periods. It suggests a major mismatch of expectations between the business and IT. It is good that this is recognized and the SLA re-negotiated, but it is not good that this is necessary.
Specification:	If a SLA has been set badly then it will be impossible to meet and a discussion with the customer will be needed to rectify the SLA setting. This metric measures this problem.
Justification:	Though this is expected to be low - or nil where SLAs are properly concluded, it is important to keep track of any SLAs that require substantial renegotiation. Good SLAs take into account that customers will have some uncontrolled additional requirements to agreed serives, due to changing business environments. The IT services organization should be ready to absorb these business capacity changes and SLAs should cover their consequences.
Audience:	Process Owner, IT Management, SLA Process Owner, Business Customer, Team Members, SIP Process Owner
Constraints:	None
Danger value:	4
Target value:	2
Possible values:	0-100

Metric:	**Number of SLA reviews completed on time {reviews}**
Description:	Reviews are important and must include information that might lead to the SLA being re-negotiated. These reviews must, however, be concluded in good time. SLAs that are under review for extended periods of time are a business risk.
Specification:	All SLAs should have a renewal date. The review date should be set to complete a fixed period before this (maybe 1 month), and the completion of the review is measured against this.
Justification:	Reducing the risk of long review periods or of reviews being opened, but not concluded.
Audience:	Process Owner, IT Management, SLA Process Owner, Team Members, SIP Process Owner

Constraints:	No
Danger value:	90
Target value:	95
Possible values:	999999

Metric:	**Number of SLA breaches caused by third party support contracts {incidents}**
Description:	This figure can help in negotiating improved services from third parties. It is also necessary to provide the business with evidence that the Underpinnning Contracts are being managed effectively.
Specification:	All incidents that breach SLA that are caused by third parties will show this in the closing information so that this can be reported here.
Justification:	Unless the effectiveness of delivery against Underpinning Contrats is measured, there is no way to be certain that they are being effective. The measure of all incidents caused by third parties is important, but more to Availability Management than to Service Level Management.
Audience:	Process Owner, IT Management, SLA Process Owner, Team Members, SIP Process Owner
Constraints:	No
Danger value:	5
Target value:	2
Possible values:	999999

Metric:	**Service Delivery costs {cost}**
Description:	Whatever the currency, 100 is representing the target value, so 2% of over that is seen as the danger area.
Specification:	This metric will eventually be measured with considerable accuracy. An easy way to get an approximation is to take the whole Service Delivery organization cost, then divide it by the number of man-hours available - this gives a cost per man-hour. Then the number of hours spent on Service Delivery can be estimated from the time spent on calls and work orders and mapped to cost.
Justification:	Though charging is not a standard objective of Service Management, costing is. It is important to have control over costs and Service Level Management is an important source of this control.
Audience:	Process Owner, IT Management, SLA Process Owner, Business Customer, Team Members, SIP Process Owner
Constraints:	This may not be possible to collect before costing is implemented.
Danger value:	102
Target value:	100
Possible values:	999999

Metric:	**Number of services not covered by SLA {services}**
Description:	Services ought not to exist unless covered by an SLA - otherwise there is no evidence that they are required for the business. Over time, though, SLAs must be re-negotiated and new services are introduced so this will vary over time.
Specification:	This will reduce as SLA management is introduced; the final aim is to cover all services.
Justification:	This is a measure of the span of control of the SLA process. If a large number of services do not have SLAs agreed and signed off then Service Level Management does not have control over the level of delivery.
Audience:	Process Owner, IT Management, SLA Process Owner, Business Customer, Team Members, SIP Process Owner
Constraints:	None
Danger value:	15
Target value:	10
Possible values:	999999

Metric:	**Number of OLAs and Underpinning Contracts (UCs) not yet agreed upon {OLA/UCs}**
Description:	Operational Level Agreements and Underpinning Contracts will be negotiated and this number will grow as Service Level Management is extended to suppliers. This is, effectively, a measure of the productivity of this process. Specification: A measure of OLAs and Underpinning Contracts that are not yet completed and signed off.
Justification:	Without this measure there is a danger that OLAs and UCs will be discussed but final agreement on difficult issues not reached. There is a danger that an SLA will be concluded without the necessary support from the appropriate OLA and UC agreements.
Audience:	Process Owner, IT Management, SLA Process Owner, Team Members, SIP Process Owner
Constraints:	No
Danger value:	40
Target value:	25
Possible values:	999999

Metric:	**Customer Satisfaction {satisfaction}**
Description:	Customer Satisfaction as measured by the process most closely associated with this one.
Specification:	Customer Satisfaction metric as described in the Process Relationship diagram.
Justification:	This is a subjective, but genuine, measure of the quality of the output of a process.
Audience:	Process Owner, IT Management, SLA Process Owner, Business Customer, Team Members, SIP Process Owner

Constraints:	No
Danger value:	< 3
Target value:	4
Possible values:	0-5

Metric:	**SLR -> SLA turnaround {days}**
Description:	This measures the time from creation of an SLR to final acceptance of an SLA.
Specification:	The turnaround time is the time it takes to turn an SLR from first creation into and signed-off SLA.
Justification:	This time is clearly affected by the speed with which the appropriate business unit can respond, as well as by the efficiency of the SLA process. However, over time, the ability to communicate, negotiate and close SLA negotiations ought to improve. This metric measures the improvement.
Audience:	Process Owner, IT Management, SLA Process Owner, Business Customer, Team Members, SIP Process Owner
Constraints:	No
Danger value:	60 days
Target value:	30 days
Possible values:	999999

H Metrics for Problem Management

The **goal** of **Problem Management** is to minimize the adverse business impact of incidents that are caused by errors within the IT infrastructure, and to prevent recurrence of incidents related to these errors. In order to achieve this goal, Problem Management seeks to get to the root cause of incidents and then initiate actions to improve or correct the situation.

(OGC ITIL Best Practice for Service Support)

Mission Statement: To minimize the disruption of IT services by organising IT resources to resolve problems according to business needs, preventing them from recurring and recording information that will improve the way in which IT deals with problems, resulting in higher levels of availability and productivity.

Process owner: Problem Manager

Metric Objective: to determine problems that are related to (potential) service disruptions and to minimize their effect or remove them entirely as a cause of disruptions.

Metric:	**Number of problems closed {problem}**
Description:	This is a measure of activity, but also of effectiveness.
Specification:	The number of problem records closed.
Justification:	Problems can take a long time to solve, however, if the rate of closing problems is high, it is an indication that the process is being effective.
Audience:	Process Owner, IT Management, SLA Process Owner, Business Customer, Team Members, SIP Process Owner
Constraints:	None
Danger value:	10
Target value:	20
Possible values:	999999

Metric:	**Number of incidents resolved by Known Errors {incidents}**
Description:	Incidents closed by solutions that were registered with Known Errors save time and re-work as well as keeping customer service levels high.
Specification:	The number of resolved incidents should increase.
Justification:	The Known Error DB is the primary communications path between Problem and Incident Management. If it is properly maintained and well produced so that it is easy to use then that will be reflected by this metric.
Audience:	Process Owner, IT Management, SLA Process Owner, Business Customer, Team Members, SIP Process Owner

Constraints:	A Known Error DB must be in place and each incident solved by a solution or work-around that was registered with a Known Error should be logged as such. Whether a Danger Value is higher or lower than a Target Value will depend upon local conditions. Therefore it might be wise to interpret the metric as "Number of incidents resolved by Known Errors, relative to all resolved incidents".
Danger value:	20
Target value:	50
Possible values:	999999

Metric:	**Total number of incidents {incidents}**
Description:	Incidents are caused by problems - if the problems are removed, then the number of incidents will reduce.
Specification:	This, and Customer Satisfaction, are the main measures of Problem Management success.
Justification:	The reduction of this measure is the prime means of establishing the contribution from Problem Management.
Audience:	Process Owner, IT Management, SLA Process Owner, Business Customer, Team Members, SIP Process Owner
Constraints:	The IT services organization must have agreed with its customers that disruptions caused by the customer are not logged as incidents. It is important to realize that this number can increase or decrease for reasons unconnected with Problem Management (users confidence or lack of it in the Service Desk, for example), so cannot be utterly relied upon, but must be used in conjunction with other metrics to understand what has caused the change. Any big changes in this metric ought to lead to an investigation, by Problem Management, to understand the reason.
Danger value:	400
Target value:	200
Possible values:	999999

Metric:	**Total user downtime {time}**
Description:	Though this is really a measure of availability, it is also a measure of the effectiveness of Problem Management - if problems are removed quickly and efficiently then users will experience much lower levels of downtime.
Specification:	This can be measured in hours by summarizing the time to solve incidents over all affected users during SLA hours.
Justification:	This is a customer facing measure and gives a direct picture of how disruptive unsolved problems are.
Audience:	Process Owner, IT Management, SLA Process Owner, Business Customer, Team Members, SIP Process Owner
Constraints:	The IT services organization must have agreed with its customers that disruptions caused by the customer are not logged as incidents.
Danger value:	200
Target value:	100
Possible values:	999999

Metric:	**Number of RFCs raised by Problem Management {RFCs}**
Description:	RFCs raised by Problem Management connected to problems.
Specification:	The number of requests for change made.
Justification:	Each RFC raised by Problem Management in response to a problem is a aimed at realizing a solution. So this is a direct measure of the output of the process.
Audience:	Process Owner, IT Management, SLA Process Owner, Business Customer, Team Members, SIP Process Owner
Constraints:	None
Danger value:	10
Target value:	20
Possible values:	999999

Metric:	**Average number of open problems {problems}**
Description:	Open problems reflect the current workload of Problem Management. This is an important measure to track against problems solved. If the number of open problems becomes too large then effectiveness is in danger.
Specification:	The average number of open problems.
Justification:	Some problems will be open a long time, but this gives a picture of how effectively the workload is being managed.
Audience:	Process Owner, IT Management, SLA Process Owner, Business Customer, Team Members, SIP Process Owner
Constraints:	None
Danger value:	40
Target value:	25
Possible values:	999999

Metric:	**Average time to close a problem {time}**
Description:	Problems can take a long time to be solved. Monitoring may be necessary for weeks, before enough data are collected to find a diagnose. If problems are open for very long periods on average, this could relate to an ineffective process.
Specification:	Time from problem creation to problem close for problems closed this period (time in hours, days or minutes).
Justification:	If this figure reduces over time, it is an indication that better tools, training and processes are being used. If it increases then it is advance warning that Problem Management might be under-resourced.
Audience:	Process Owner, IT Management, SLA Process Owner, Business Customer, Team Members, SIP Process Owner
Constraints:	When a long-outstanding problem is closed, this could cause this metric to jump making the trend difficult to measure. So it might be sensible to exclude problems that have been open longer than a month from the measure.
Danger value:	5
Target value:	3
Possible values:	999999

Metric:	**Percentage of incidents not linked to problems {%incidents}**
Description:	This shows incidents that have not yet been examined by Problem Management.
Specification:	The percentage of incidents that are not linked to a problem record - this can be measured once a day and averaged over the week, or an average could be taken every hour.
Justification:	All incidents are caused by problems (though not all Service Calls are). When they are linked to a problem it shows that ultimate resolution is in the hands of Problem Management. A very high percentage of unlinked incidents shows inefficiencies in Problem Management and might be an indication of a lack of resources.
Audience:	Process Owner, IT Management, SLA Process Owner, Business Customer, Team Members, SIP Process Owner
Constraints:	There is a limit to the amount of energy that should be put in determining the root cause of incidents. Only (groups of) incidents that cause serious damage to the business should be investigated, based on a business case approach.
Danger value:	40
Target value:	25
Possible values:	0-100

Metric:	**Number of problems that missed target resolution time {problems}**
Description:	Just as with incidents, problems are given target solution times based on SLA and urgency of the associated incidents. This measures how effective Problem Management is at meeting this objective.
Specification:	The number of problems that have exceeded the target solution date and been escalated.
Justification:	This gives a picture of how many serious problems exist. If our process includes an 'investigation' or 'resolution' phase the time spent in these can be made a target in order to identify longer term problems for separate treatment whilst dealing with standard ones in a timely manner. This is done so that escalation of problem resolution can be used to determine of more time should be spent on a particularly stubborn problem (that might have low impact) rather than on other, less interesting, medium impact problems. The issue is balancing resources with urgency, impact and duration - the urgency and impact can increase with duration so more resources may need to be allocated to stubborn problems. This can only be investigated if there are some targets and some escalation points.
Audience:	Process Owner, IT Management, SLA Process Owner, Business Customer, Team Members, SIP Process Owner
Constraints:	None
Danger value:	5
Target value:	2
Possible values:	999999

Metric:	**Customer Satisfaction {satisfaction}**
Description:	Customer Satisfaction as measured by the process(es) most closely associated with this one.
Specification:	Customer Satisfaction metric as described in the Process Relationship diagram.
Justification:	This is a subjective, but genuine, measure of the quality of the output of a process.
Audience:	Process Owner, IT Management, SLA Process Owner, Business Customer, Team Members, SIP Process Owner
Constraints:	No
Danger value:	< 3
Target value:	4
Possible values:	0-5

Metric Objective: *To assist Problem Management in identifying trends.*

Metric:	**Top 5 categories of incidents reported for the period {incidents}**
Description:	A pie chart which shows the 5 highest percentages of categories of calls received in the reporting period. When this is done for every reporting period, trends can be observed and possible problem areas identified for further analysis.
Specification:	The number of incident tickets in each category divided by the total number of tickets for the period multiplied by 100. Out of this list, the top 5 categories depicted in a pie chart.
Justification:	Incident Management can be used effectively to identify trends in incident occurrence. Some areas may show a consistently high percentage of incidents (e.g. email, application bugs), which in turn contributes to prioritization and proactive problem management.
Audience:	Process Owner, Team Members, SIP Process Owner, Problem Management
Constraints:	This cannot be included in the consolidated metrics, it is an informative internal metric, not a process metric.
Danger value:	N/A
Target value:	N/A
Possible values:	N/A

Metric Objective: *To reduce number of incidents reported and increase support effectiveness.*

Metric:	**Number of incidents for which the solution is user training {incidents}**
Description:	Just as errors of infrastructure result in incidents, so does lack of user knowledge in using applications. A considerable percentage of incidents may be avoided by just training the users.

Specification:	Number of calls where the solution says 'user training required' in a particular incident category.
Justification:	An efficient incident and problem management process should also identify how incidents can be reduced by providing user training; otherwise the requirement for support members would rise disproportionately.
Audience:	Process Owner, IT Management, SLA Process Owner, Business Customer, Team Members, SIP Process Owner
Constraints:	The solution must record the training requirement.
Danger value:	=> 25 in a particular category would probably warrant a training session
Target value:	0
Possible values:	99999

Metric Objective: *To discover what are the outstanding costs of quality in problem management.*

Metric:	**Cost of solving a problem {cost}**
Description:	The total amount of costs the solving of a given problem has costed.
Specification:	Measure staff hours, material costs and other issues that solving the problem has involved.
Justification:	Problem Management is a quality management process. Quality has its price. For all existing problems a business case should be made to determine whether or not to correct the problem. This is often based on estimates. The estimates could become much more accurate with the help of practice-proven measurements of the cost of solving similar problems. Please note that Change Management is responsible and will make the decisions about wether to solve a problem and pay the costs or not.
Audience:	Process Owner, IT Management, SLA Process Owner, Business Customer, Team Members, SIP Process Owner
Constraints:	Problem Managers will need to document everything they do very precisely, to ensure all actions will be trackable to specific problems.
Danger value:	Depends on the problem: the solving of a problem should never cost more than it yields.
Target value:	Make the solution of the problem profitable.
Possible values:	Theoretically unlimited

I Metrics for Financial Management for IT services

> The **goal** of **Financial Management for IT services** is to provide cost-effective stewardship of the IT assets and resources used in providing IT services. (OGC ITIL Best Practice for Service Support)

> **Mission Statement:** To manage IT infrastructure costs and to provide a sound basis for business decisions relating to IT by identifying and accounting for the costs of delivering services, and where feasible by recovering costs in an equitable manner.

> **Process owner:** IT Manager

> **Metric Objective:** To manage IT infrastructure costs and to provide a sound basis for business decisions relating to IT by identifying and accounting for the costs of delivering services, and where feasible by recovering costs in an equitable manner.

Metric:	Percentage of IT costs accounted for {%cost}
Description:	The scope of current costing. The CMDB will provide some costs from the Asset DB - these can be checked against the records kept by accounts. Over time the CMDB will be more and more accurate.
Specification:	Ultimately all IT costs, direct and indirect, will be included. To being with operating expenses such as salaries, telephones and electricity will be known. This can be calculated with help from the accounting department.
Justification:	The wider the scope, the better.
Audience:	Process Owner, IT Management, SLA Process Owner, Business Customer, Team Members, SIP Process Owner
Constraints:	None
Danger value:	50
Target value:	70
Possible values:	0-100

Metric:	Number of changes made to charging algorithm {changes}
Description:	How close we are to a stable system.
Specification:	The number of changes made to the algorithm. Even if real charging is not being carried out, it is useful to have a charging algorithm and to test it regularly for reasonableness.
Justification:	Eventually we would desire this to be stable because we have accurate models - until then it is a good sign that the matter is being actively managed.
Audience:	Process Owner, IT Management, SLA Process Owner, Business Customer, Team Members, SIP Process Owner

Constraints:	None
Danger value:	10
Target value:	3
Possible values:	999999

Metric:	**Delay in production of financial report {days}**
Description:	How long it takes to get the report out.
Specification:	A date is set for the production of the regular financial report; this indicates slippage from this date.
Justification:	Once the process is mature, the report will be on time. Until then, this is a good mark of how well it is improving.
Audience:	Process Owner, IT Management, SLA Process Owner, Business Customer, Team Members, SIP Process Owner
Constraints:	None
Danger value:	2
Target value:	1
Possible values:	999999

Metric:	**Delay in production of monthly forecast {days}**
Description:	Delay measured in days.
Specification:	Each month the forecast for the next financial figures is produced.
Justification:	When mature these will be on time - until then this is a test of how well the process is maturing.
Audience:	Process Owner, IT Management, SLA Process Owner, Business Customer, Team Members, SIP Process Owner
Constraints:	None
Danger value:	2
Target value:	1
Possible values:	999999

Metric:	**Percentage of accuracy of the last financial forecast {%cost}**
Description:	Forecast accuracy as a percentage.
Specification:	This measures: abs(financial actuals - financial forecast) / financial actuals* 100 over the last period
Justification:	This is a measure of how well Financial Management is doing.
Audience:	Process Owner, IT Management, SLA Process Owner, Business Customer, Team Members, SIP Process Owner
Constraints:	None
Danger value:	80
Target value:	85
Possible values:	0-100

Metric:	**Percentage of accuracy of financial forecast for the previous quarter {%cost}**
Description:	This is a rolling measure of previous forecasts to actuals.
Specification:	This measures: abs(financial actuals - financial forecast) / financial actuals* 100 over the last period (quarter)
Justification:	Capacity Management is largely responsible for future estimates and forecasts. However, it relies upon financial data to make these accurate, so it makes sense for Financial Management to be responsible for this metric. This also has the effect of encouraging Financial Management to work closely with Capacity Management to ensure that this improves.
Audience:	Process Owner, IT Management, SLA Process Owner, Business Customer, Team Members, SIP Process Owner
Constraints:	None
Danger value:	60
Target value:	75
Possible values:	0-100

Metric:	**Total Cost of Ownership (TCO) of IT {cost}**
Description:	As measured from Financial Management models and the CMDB.
Specification:	This is how much it costs the business to own IT. It includes all financial costs including wages, depreciation, equipment, and infrastructure. Over time, the objective is for this to decrease.
Justification:	Over time the aim of Financial Management to reduce this.
Audience:	Process Owner, IT Management, SLA Process Owner, Business Customer, Team Members, SIP Process Owner
Constraints:	None
Danger value:	50
Target value:	10
Possible values:	999999

Metric:	**Number of complaints regarding IT cost {complaints}**
Description:	Most of this will be found in Service Desk complaints and in regular SLA meetings.
Specification:	Complaints raised as complaints by the Service Desk or tabled at SLA meetings must be recorded to be tracked.
Justification:	Either Financial Management is not communicating the reason for certain costs, or the reasons have been found unconvincing. In either case it suggests that the principles of Financial Management need further attention.
Audience:	Process Owner, IT Management, SLA Process Owner, Business Customer, Team Members, SIP Process Owner
Constraints:	None
Danger value:	10
Target value:	5
Possible values:	999999

Metric:	**Number of questions regarding IT cost {queries}**
Description:	Most of this will be found in Service Desk questions and in regular SLA meetings.
Specification:	Questions raised as complaints by the Service Desk or tabled at SLA meetings must be recorded to be tracked.
Justification:	Either Financial Management is not communicating the reason for certain costs, or the reasons have been found unconvincing. In either case it suggests that the principles of Financial Management need further attention.
Audience:	Process Owner, IT Management, SLA Process Owner, Business Customer, Team Members, SIP Process Owner
Constraints:	None
Danger value:	40
Target value:	30
Possible values:	999999

Metric Objective: To provide effective Financial Management for IT Service Management.

Metric:	**Customer Satisfaction {satisfaction}**
Description:	Customer Satisfaction with Financial Management as measured by internal process response.
Specification:	Customer Satisfaction as measured by the Process Relationship diagram. Justification: This is a measure of the effectiveness of Financial Management.
Audience:	Process Owner, IT Management, SLA Process Owner, Business Customer, Team Members, SIP Process Owner
Constraints:	None
Danger value:	< 3
Target value:	4
Possible values:	0-5

J   Metrics for Capacity Management

The **goal** of **Capacity Management** is to ensure that cost justifiable IT capacity always exists and that it is matched to the current and future identified needs of the business. (OGC ITIL Best Practice for Service Support)

Mission Statement: To ensure the best use of the appropriate IT infrastructure to meet business needs currently and in the future through a proper understanding of both business and infrastructure requirements.

Process owner: Capacity Manager

Metric Objective: To provide effective Capacity Management.

Metric:	Number of SLA breaches because of poor service performance {SLA breaches}
Description:	Capacity Management has the task of ensuring that SLA performance times are not exceeded as a result of inadequate capacity. If possible, only incidents related to capacity ought to be measured, but this depends on mature Incident and Problem Management processes.
Specification:	Call response time exceeded, or application response time, for example.
Justification:	Capacity Management has the job of anticipating potential service disruption because of capacity issues - this is a measure of how effective this job is being done.
Audience:	Process Owner, IT Management, SLA Process Owner, Business Customer, Team Members, SIP Process Owner
Constraints:	Where possible only capacity related incidents ought to be counted.
Danger value:	2
Target value:	0
Possible values:	999999

Metric Objective: To provide effective Resource Capacity Management.

Metric:	Number of SLA breaches because of poor component performance {SLA breaches}
Description:	Component failures as a result of performance or other capacity related problems.
Specification:	System performance poor, for example.
Justification:	Resource Capacity Management has the responsibility to ensure that failures as a result of insufficient capacity are kept to a minimum.
Audience:	Process Owner, IT Management, SLA Process Owner, Business Customer, Team Members, SIP Process Owner
Constraints:	If possible only incidents that are related directly to capacity issues should be included.

Danger value:	2
Target value:	0
Possible values:	999999

Metric Objective: *To provide sufficient capacity to deliver agreed services to agreed service levels.*

Metric:	**Number of incidents as a result of poor performance {incidents}**
Description:	Only performance related incidents are included. Monitoring and tuning coupled with trend analysis ought to ensure that performance related incidents do not occur.
Specification:	Incident and Problem Management will need to have performance as a possible closing cause - and have good processes for making the decision that this is the cause. This metric is measured from that closing disposition.
Justification:	This is a direct measure of effective Capacity Management.
Audience:	Process Owner, IT Management, SLA Process Owner, Business Customer, Team Members, SIP Process Owner
Constraints:	None
Danger value:	10
Target value:	5
Possible values:	999999

Metric Objective: *To produce a cost-effective Capacity Plan.*

Metric:	**Cost of production of Capacity Plan {cost}**
Description:	Total planning costs. This is measured separately from other standard running costs, so work will need to be done with Financial Management to establish how these costs can be monitored regularly.
Specification:	Man-hours spent this planning period as well as the cost of tools et cetera.
Justification:	Capacity Management ought to be producing Capacity Plans to take into account future trends and business needs. These have to be produced costeffectively. So this measure establishes both that the plans are being produced and that they are not involving too many resources.
Audience:	Process Owner, IT Management, SLA Process Owner, Team Members, SIP Process Owner
Constraints:	Financial Management needs to be fairly sophisticated to be able to produce this metric.
Danger value:	30
Target value:	10
Possible values:	999999

Metric:	**Number of unplanned purchases of performance related hardware {cost}**
Description:	Any purchase required for performance related matters is unplanned unless it is listed in the Capacity Plan.
Specification:	This would include extra RAM, Disc, CPU, systems or networks that are bought to solve performance problems that were not planned as part of the Capacity Plan. Mark by item product number or by cost.
Justification:	Capacity Management ought to be planning purchases in advance of requirements, in response to measured trends and known business plans. This checks that unplanned purchases are reducing in response to good planning.
Audience:	Process Owner, IT Management, SLA Process Owner, Team Members, SIP Process Owner
Constraints:	None
Danger value:	15
Target value:	10
Possible values:	999999

Metric:	**Percentage of accuracy of plan of forecast expenditure {%expenditure}**
Description:	How much spending exceeds plans based on capacity. Changes as a result of new business requirements should be reflected in Capacity Management scenarios and the planned expenditure adjusted to reflect these.
Specification:	abs(Period Planned expenditure - Period Actual Expenditure)/Planned Expenditure * 100 over a specified period
Justification:	Capacity Management produces Capacity Plans that forecast expenditure against business plans. This is a measure of the accuracy of those plans.
Audience:	Process Owner, IT Management, SLA Process Owner, Team Members, SIP Process Owner
Constraints:	Financial Management needs to be fairly sophisticated to get an accurate picture of this.
Danger value:	80
Target value:	90
Possible values:	0-100

Metric:	**Percentage of over-capacity of IT {%capacity}**
Description:	Performance levels, Disc, Memory, CPU, Network Bandwidth and so forth, can all be monitored against an appropriate capacity policy. Overcapacity can be recorded and summed to provide this metric. Over time it ought to be managed downwards.
Specification:	This can be measured by auditing performance levels of key CIs. Capacity is defined in the Capacity Management Plan.
Justification:	Capacity Management is responsible for providing effective capacity - not too much, which is expensive.
Audience:	Process Owner, IT Management, SLA Process Owner, Business Customer, Team Members, SIP Process Owner
Constraints:	None
Danger value:	30
Target value:	20
Possible values:	0-100

Metric:	**Percentage of CIs monitored for performance {%CIs}**
Description:	If monitoring is turned off, for any reason, this should cause an event that ought to trigger this metric. If performance monitoring is not on at key servers, Capacity Management is, effectively, blind to trends.
Specification:	A measure of CIs that have performance monitoring turned on. This can be defined in more detail to exclude those CIs that are known not to be directly relevant to capacity monitoring.
Justification:	Capacity Management must understand the current capacity levels and the trends in these levels. This can only be done with effective monitoring of CIs in the infrastructure.
Audience:	Process Owner, IT Management, SLA Process Owner, Team Members, SIP Process Owner
Constraints:	None
Danger value:	60
Target value:	70
Possible values:	0-100

Metric:	**Percentage overall Business Load of Expected Business Load {%Business Load}**
Description:	Expected Business Load is defined in the Capacity Management Plan, as is the measure of 'Business Load' for this metric.
Specification:	A measure of how much the overall Business Load on IT is relative to that anticipated in the Capacity Management Plan.
Justification:	Capacity Management must understand the current capacity levels and the trends in these levels. These must be tied to business capacity plans so that proper forecasts can be made and errors in current forecasts understood.
Audience:	Process Owner, IT Management, SLA Process Owner, Business Customer, Team Members, SIP Process Owner
Constraints:	None
Danger value:	85
Target value:	80
Possible values:	0-100%

Metric:	**Customer Satisfaction {satisfaction}**
Description:	Customer Satisfaction
Specification:	Customer Satisfaction measured according to the Process Relationship diagram.
Justification:	This is required to ensure that effective process outputs are produced.
Audience:	Process Owner, IT Management, SLA Process Owner, Business Customer, Team Members, SIP Process Owner
Constraints:	None
Danger value:	< 3
Target value:	4
Possible values:	0-5

K   Metrics for IT Service Continuity Management

The **goal** of **IT Service Continuity Management** is to support the overall Business Continuity Management process, by ensuring that the required IT technical and services facilities (including computer systems, networks, applications, telecommunications, technical support and Service Desk) can be recovered within required, and agreed, business timescales.

(OGC ITIL Best Practice for Service Support)

Mission Statement: To support the overall Business Continuity Management process by ensuring that the required IT technical and services facilities can be recovered within the required and agreed business time scales.

Process owner: Continuity Manager

Metric Objective: To support the overall Business Continuity Management process by ensuring that the required IT technical and services facilities can be recovered within the required and agreed business time scales.

Metric:	**Number of services not covered by IT Service Continuity (ITSC) plan {services}**
Description:	Every service and SLA will have links to the ITSC - even if they are to say that the particular service will not be covered in the event of an emergency.
Specification:	ITSC = IT Service Continuity
Justification:	If any service is not part of the ITSC plan it is under risk. This metric ensures that any services at risk are monitored and dealt with.
Audience:	Process Owner, IT Management, SLA Process Owner, Business Customer, Team Members, SIP Process Owner
Constraints:	None
Danger value:	10
Target value:	5
Possible values:	999999

Metric:	**Delay in ITSC plan completion/update {days}**
Description:	This is a measure of business risk. The plan completion and update dates must be under document control and that is where they are measured.
Specification:	Measured in days, this is the time delay from the date the plan or update was due (if it was this month) and the date delivered.
Justification:	If the plan is incomplete then there is a risk that recovery will not be complete either. This measure makes sure that the plans are not incomplete for too long.

Audience:	Process Owner, IT Management, SLA Process Owner, Team Members, SIP Process Owner
Constraints:	None
Danger value:	5
Target value:	1
Possible values:	999999

Metric:	**Delay in ITSC test date {days}**
Description:	This is measured from the ITSC plan that is under document control.
Specification:	Measured in days, this is the time delay from the date the test was due (if it was this month) and the date delivered.
Justification:	There are many possible reasons for these delays. Most commonly individuals taking part in the test are required elsewhere in the business. This delay puts the business at risk and must be highlighted to ensure that repeated delays do not result in a serious delay in the readiness of the plan.
Audience:	Process Owner, IT Management, SLA Process Owner, Team Members, SIP Process Owner
Constraints:	None
Danger value:	10
Target value:	5
Possible values:	999999

Metric:	**Number of issues raised by last test still to be addressed {issues}**
Description:	The plan, issues and actions are all under document control, so it is there that they are measured.
Specification:	Each test of the ITSC plan will give rise to some issues that must be addressed to reduce risk. The number of issues that remain to be addressed this period is measured here.
Justification:	The plan is not working as long as there are unaddressed issues. So, for business risk to be kept low, this metric must be monitored carefully.
Audience:	Process Owner, IT Management, SLA Process Owner, Team Members, SIP Process Owner
Constraints:	None
Danger value:	10
Target value:	5
Possible values:	999999

Metric:	**Results from continuity awareness survey - Percentage of pass {%passes}**
Description:	A survey can be carried out regularly with a different audience so that the same people are only surveyed every year or eighteen months.
Specification:	All IT must be aware of the business impact, needs and requirements. This survey to test the level of awareness can be conducted regulalrly (e.g. monthly) on different members of IT. The score is a measure of the level of awareness.

Justification:	This survey identifies how well the Communications Plan is working. Poor results indicate an alteration in the method, presentation or delivery of communication and possibly the need for specific training courses or presentations to improve awareness.
Audience:	Process Owner, IT Management, SLA Process Owner, Team Members, SIP Process Owner
Constraints:	None
Danger value:	90
Target value:	95
Possible values:	0-100

Metric:	**Number of issues identified this period that threaten the ITSC plan {issues}**
Description:	These issues are measured through document control where they are listed along with their dates of resolution and action plans.
Specification:	The ITSC plan requires access to equipment, backup, off-site locations and personnel. The ITSC manager must identify any issues that exist this month that impede this access. For example, staff shortages because of illness might be a threat to the continuity plan.
Justification:	Various things can give rise to issues with business continuity plans. That is a good thing. What is important, though, is that these issues are tracked and acted upon as this metric measures.
Audience:	Process Owner, IT Management, SLA Process Owner, Team Members, SIP Process Owner
Constraints:	None
Danger value:	10
Target value:	2
Possible values:	999999

Metric:	**Number of targeted communications circulated {communications}**
Description:	This is measured by reference to document control where these communications must be kept.
Specification:	Each IT Service area and business area must know what its role in the ITSC plan is. Communications can be targeted at each area and sent to one each period to ensure preparedness. This metric ensures that this is being done.
Justification:	If the business is not aware of continuity requirements then it cannot be expected to know how to behave in the case of an emergency. These communications ensure that everybody is aware of what the current instructions are.
Audience:	Process Owner, IT Management, SLA Process Owner, Team Members, SIP Process Owner
Constraints:	None
Danger value:	0
Target value:	1
Possible values:	999999

Metric:	**Number of wrong entries in crisis control team directory {contacts}**
Description:	Ideally a random time and a random selection of contacts is selected and their validity is tested by an independent agent - maybe the Service Desk.
Specification:	Once per period all the contact information can be checked for accuracy and this metric reported - the directory can be updated at the same time.
Justification:	If the contact details are wrong, it shows that change control and configuration control are not operating effectively in managing the ITSC plan. It also shows that the right people will not be contacted in the event of an emergency which could have a serious impact on the ability to recover.
Audience:	Process Owner, IT Management, SLA Process Owner, Team Members, SIP Process Owner
Constraints:	None
Danger value:	1
Target value:	0
Possible values:	999999

Metric:	**Delay in preparedness of recovery site {time}**
Description:	This measure of preparedness is a measure of business risk.
Specification:	The recovery site can be contacted at a random time each period to check how long it would take the facility to be available. The difference between this and the expected time is the delay reported here.
Justification:	If business risk is not measured then it cannot be reduced. This metric ensures that there is a regular and frequent test that recovery is not compromised by problems with the recovery site. If this was often shown to be high then another recovery site might be chosen.
Audience:	Process Owner, IT Management, SLA Process Owner, Team Members, SIP Process Owner
Constraints:	None
Danger value:	1
Target value:	0
Possible values:	999999

Metric:	**Customer Satisfaction {satisfaction}**
Description:	This is not measured against particular disasters, which we all hope do not happen, but against business satisfaction with the planning and the process for keeping the plans valid.
Specification:	Measured in relation to the Process Relationship diagram.
Justification:	IT Service Continuity is a planning process that crosses all business processes and entities. It is important that users who are part of the process are satisfied with it in terms of how it affects them.
Audience:	Process Owner, IT Management, SLA Process Owner, Business Customer, Team Members, SIP Process Owner
Constraints:	None
Danger value:	< 3
Target value:	4
Possible values:	0-5

L   Metrics for Availability Management

The **goal** of **Availability Management** is to optimize the capability of the IT infrastructure, services and supporting organization, to deliver a cost effective and sustained level of availability that enables the business to satisfy its business objectives.

(OGC ITIL Best Practice for Service Support)

Mission Statement: To ensure the delivery of IT services where, when and to whom they are required, by planning and building a reliable and maintainable infrastructure and maintaining key support and supply relationships according to service requirements.

Process owner: Availability Manager

Metric Objective: To ensure the delivery of IT services where, when and to whom they are required, by planning and building a reliable and maintainable infrastructure and maintaining key support and supply relationships according to service requirements.

Metric:	Downtime, unavailability of services {minutes}
Description:	Any time a service is not available during contracted hours.
Specification:	Time a service was down in minutes. This is a simple measure of the availability of services.
Justification:	This is a pure measure of total availability.
Audience:	Process Owner, IT Management, SLA Process Owner, Business Customer, Team Members, SIP Process Owner
Constraints:	It is very hard to define when a service is available, especially when there are multiple users, and multiple functions combined in one service. Imagine a service to 1000 end users and two users can't access the service at a certain moment. Is the service down? Partially down? Not down? The contracted service levels must be defined in such a way that the IT services organization can always determine to what extent a service was available or not.
Danger value:	40
Target value:	20
Possible values:	999999

Metric:	**Unavailability of component {minutes}**
Description:	Component level downtime - measured by Operations at the level of a Managed Object (MO), not a CI. Best taken from the Operations monitoring tool.
Specification:	Time a component was down.
Justification:	Though components (particularly redundant ones) may go down without affecting the service, if they are down then the service is under increased vulnerability to further outages. For this reason component, as well as service, reliability are important.
Audience:	Process Owner, IT Management, SLA Process Owner, Business Customer, Team Members, SIP Process Owner
Constraints:	This metric is not directly related to service levels, but indirectly it is a threat to agreed service levels. It should only be used in the context of OLAs or UCs.
Danger value:	60
Target value:	30
Possible values:	999999

Metric:	**Incident detection time {minutes}**
Description:	Time before an incident is detected.
Specification:	Time that is lost after the start of an incident before it is discovered. Could be measured as a set of values in a table or diagram, or as a mean.
Justification:	To keep incident restoration as quick as possible, it is important to detect any incident as soon as possible. Close monitoring can provide this, preferably automated.
Audience:	Process Owner, IT Management, SLA Process Owner, Business Customer, Team Members, SIP Process Owner
Constraints:	None
Danger value:	4
Target value:	1
Possible values:	999999

Metric:	**Incident response time {minutes}**
Description:	Time after detection, before first repair action is taken.
Specification:	Could be measured as a set of values in a table or diagram, or as a mean.
Justification:	Before any action can be taken to repair the incident, a diagnose ie required. Getting to the diagnose quickly can be supported by skilled helpdesks, knowledge bases, et cetera.
Audience:	Process Owner, IT Management, SLA Process Owner, Business Customer, Team Members, SIP Process Owner
Constraints:	None
Danger value: 1	0
Target value:	5
Possible values:	999999

Metric:	**Incident repair time {minutes}**
Description:	Time after diagnose, before an incident is repaired.
Specification:	Time that is spent on actual repair, after a diagnose has been made. Could be measured as a set of values in a table or diagram, or as a mean.
Justification:	To resolve an incident as quick as possible, it is important to manage the actual repair time. This time can be influenced by special arrangements e.g. by having a set of spare components at close range, or having a repair kit at location.
Audience:	Process Owner, IT Management, SLA Process Owner, Business Customer, Team Members, SIP Process Owner
Constraints:	None
Danger value:	20
Target value:	10
Possible values:	999999

Metric:	**Incident recovery time {minutes}**
Description:	Time to recover failed components.
Specification:	Time after repair, required to recover the components to their normal functions.
Justification:	Once the involved components have been repaired, they need be restored before they can contribute to the service. This can depend upon start-up times of equipment, conditions to be created, et cetera.
Audience:	Process Owner, IT Management, SLA Process Owner, Business Customer, Team Members, SIP Process Owner
Constraints:	None
Danger value:	5
Target value:	2
Possible values:	999999

Metric:	**Incident restoration time {minutes}**
Description:	Time to restore the services to the agreed level.
Specification:	Time after component recovery, required to restore the services to the agreed level.
Justification:	Once the involved components have been recovered, the service needs to be made available to the users. This can depend upon conditions to be created, data to be reset, et cetera.
Audience:	Process Owner, IT Management, SLA Process Owner, Business Customer, Team Members, SIP Process Owner
Constraints:	None
Danger value:	5
Target value:	2
Possible values:	999999

Metric:	**Incident resolution time {minutes}**
Description:	Time till recovery after detection of an incident.
Specification:	The sum of Incident response time, Incident repair time, Incident recovery time and Incident restoration time.
Justification:	In case a detailed management of response/repair/recovery/restoration is not available, this sum could be used to manage the time between detection and recovery.
Audience:	Process Owner, IT Management, SLA Process Owner, Business Customer, Team Members, SIP Process Owner
Constraints:	None
Danger value:	40
Target value:	20
Possible values:	999999

Metric:	**MTBSI (Mean Time Between System Incidents) {minutes}**
Description:	Average time between the start of subsequent incidents, indicating the level of stability of a service.
Specification:	This is the mean time between the start of subsequent incidents as measured by the Service Desk and Incident Management, measured in minutes, hours or days.
Justification:	This figure is of great importance to a good understanding of the overall 'availability' value. An availability of 99.99% measured over a period of one year could come down to 1 outage of almost 1 hour, as well as to 365 outages of almost 9 seconds - which will have a considerably different impact on the user community. The MTBSI value is an indicator of the stability aspect of availability.
Audience:	Process Owner, IT Management, SLA Process Owner, Business Customer, Team Members, SIP Process Owner
Constraints:	None
Danger value:	150
Target value:	200
Possible values:	999999

Metric:	**MTTR (Mean Time To Repair "downtime", Mean Time To Restore) {minutes}**
Description:	MTTR is a standard measure of availability, measuring the average elapsed time from the occurrence of an incident to resolution of the incident (average downtime per incident).
Specification:	This is the average time to restore a service to operational status, or average downtime per service disruption (incident).
Justification:	Measuring this by service, not component, enables the focus to be at the right level for the business.
Audience:	Process Owner, IT Management, SLA Process Owner, Business Customer, Team Members, SIP Process Owner

Constraints:	None
Danger value:	40
Target value:	20
Possible values:	999999

Metric:	**Critical time failure {minutes}**
Description:	Critical time for financial systems services might be the 27-29th of each month. This is the total outage time during these critical periods, measured in minutes.
Specification:	This is the failure of services during critical time - critical time is defined per service. For example, critical time for most e-mail could be 08.00-10.00 hrs, when people start working at the office and they need to see their emails.
Justification:	This measure of critical support time is a more acute indication of really serious problems than simple SLA breaches.
Audience:	Process Owner, IT Management, SLA Process Owner, Business Customer, Team Members, SIP Process Owner
Constraints:	None
Danger value:	40
Target value:	20
Possible values:	999999

Metric:	**Unavailability of third party services {minutes}**
Description:	Downtime of services offered to IT by third parties in minutes.
Specification:	Downtime caused by Incidents caused by third Party Services.
Justification:	Third Party downtime causing downtime to services, is a vital interest of Availability Management.
Audience:	Process Owner, IT Management, SLA Process Owner, Business Customer, Team Members, SIP Process Owner
Constraints:	None
Danger value:	120
Target value:	60
Possible values:	999999

Metric:	**Unavailability of third party components {minutes}**
Description:	This focuses on components - the ultimate source of downtime. Though the previous metric is important as it concentrates on services, this provides an important balance.
Specification:	Time a third party component was down.
Justification:	Component level trending is part of the role of Availability Management. Though components (particularly redundant ones) may go down without affecting the service, if they are down then the service is under increased vulnerability to further outages. For this reason component, as well as service, reliability are important.
Audience:	Process Owner, IT Management, SLA Process Owner, Business Customer, Team Members, SIP Process Owner

Constraints:	None
Danger value:	60
Target value:	30
Possible values:	999999

> **Metric Objective:** *To provide effective management of service and component availability.*

Metric:	**Time used to resolve unavailable services {minutes}**
Description:	The time taken to repair customer services.
Specification:	This is a measure of the man-hours expended in resolving availability issues.
Justification:	Many methods can be used to reduce repair related downtime - it is important that the success in doing this is measured. Redundant systems can reduce this and this metric can help identify which services require that measure to be taken.
Audience:	Process Owner, IT Management, SLA Process Owner, Business Customer, Team Members, SIP Process Owner
Constraints:	A good hour registration system needs to be in place.
Danger value:	60
Target value:	30
Possible values:	999999

Metric:	**Number of repeat failures {incidents}**
Description:	Number of times CIs fail repeatedly (more than once).
Specification:	This is the sum of all multiple failures on CIs.
Justification:	Part of the job of availability management is to reduce multiple failures. Its success is shown by this metric. The report, per CI, ordered by number of failures, allows availability management to select the worst performing CIs to replace, perform analysis on or otherwise work to make more available.
Audience:	Process Owner, IT Management, SLA Process Owner, Business Customer, Team Members, SIP Process Owner
Constraints:	None
Danger value:	600
Target value:	300
Possible values:	999999

M   Metrics for Security Management

The **goal** of **Security Management** is to manage information security effectively within all service activities.

Firstly, to meet the external security requirements. These result from the security requirements in the various SLAs. These external requirements for security also stem from contracts, legislation and any imposed security policy.

Secondly, to meet the internal security requirements. This is required to assure the IT service provider's own continuity. It is also necessary to simplify the Service Level Management for information security. After all, managing a large number of different SLAs is much more complex than managing a small number. Therefore, for instance, a certain basic level of security (the so-called standard security baseline) needs to be established.

Mission Statement: To manage and control the Security Management process to meet external security requirements as found in SLAs, contracts, legislation and the company security policy. To meet internal security requiremetns to assure the continuity of IT service provision.

Process owner: IT Security Manager

Metric Objective: To manage and control the Security Management process to meet external security requirements as found in SLAs, contracts, legislation and the company security policy. To meet internal security requirements to assure the continuity of IT service provision.

Metric:	Number of security related incidents {incidents}
Description:	This is based on the closing disposition of incident and call records.
Specification:	Benchmark this over time. This will depend on the level of control as well as other factors such as software quality.
Justification:	It is vital that Security Management processes are aware of the relevant incidents. Good processes will, over time, reduce the number and severity of these incidents.
Audience:	Process Owner, IT Management, SLA Process Owner, Team Members, SIP Process Owner
Constraints:	None
Danger value:	100
Target value:	50
Possible values:	999999

Metric:	**Number of security related problems closed {problems}**
Description:	This is a measure of problems closed with a closing disposition linked to it security.
Specification:	This is a measure of Problem Management process efficiency. However, Security Management has an obligation to ensure that all processes include security provisions. This metric is fundamental to understanding how good Security Management is.
Justification:	Resolution of security related problems will result in reduced numbers of incidents and improve availability.
Audience:	Process Owner, IT Management, SLA Process Owner, Team Members, SIP Process Owner
Constraints:	None
Danger value:	5
Target value:	10
Possible values:	999999

Metric:	**Number of Audit + Internal Review issues resolved {issues}**
Description:	The issue list should have resolution dates - those could be used (in addition to this metric) to trigger alarms if exceeded.
Specification:	Internal Reviews and Audits ought to show up minor issues to be resolved. These might take time; this metric ensures that progress continues towards this goal.
Justification:	Security is a long-term process of improving things. Issues raised by audits or internal reviews are important to getting it under proper control. This metric ensures that long term resolution is kept in constant focus.
Audience:	Process Owner, IT Management, SLA Process Owner, Team Members, SIP Process Owner
Constraints:	The issue list must be under document control.
Danger value:	5
Target value:	8
Possible values:	999999

Metric:	**Percentage of Reviews + Audits conducted on time {reviews/audits}**
Description:	A measure of Reviews and Audits against planned dates.
Specification:	Internal Audits or Reviews slipping can be a sign of over-work, a lack of resources or matters that are more serious. It is important that these are highly visible.
Justification:	We rely upon Internal Reviews (and to a lesser extent) Audits to highlight shortcomings in this process. It is vital that they are carried out. This ensures that they are not only carried out but also carried out timeously.
Audience:	Process Owner, IT Management, SLA Process Owner, Team Members, SIP Process Owner
Constraints:	Audit and Review plans and appointments must be under document control.
Danger value:	95
Target value:	100
Possible values:	0-100

Metric:	**Number of risks identified (warnings + new threats) {risks}**
Description:	A process must be in place to log risks that are identified - and qualify them with action to be taken. This log is measured for this metric.
Specification:	Risks and threats cannot be invented where none exist! However in any complex environment, new risks, albeit small ones, can be uncovered every week, or at least every month. That they are uncovered proves that an active Security Management process is in place.
Justification:	Security Management must be actively engaged to find new risks, or threats. This measures success: even when depending upon context, it will always be possible to identify risks.
Audience:	Process Owner, IT Management, SLA Process Owner, Team Members, SIP Process Owner
Constraints:	None
Danger value:	5
Target value:	10
Possible values:	999999

Metric:	**Percentage of SLAs with explicit security specifications {%SLAs}**
Description:	SLAs are kept in the CMDB. Each SLA has a security clause. This metric ought to check that these include more than simple boilerplate. Each SLA ought to be properly considered for any security implications. This can, crudely, be measured by comparing the security fields. Properly this ought to be a mini Audit or Internal Review task.
Specification:	If SLAs are static, this might not be a useful metric. It is important that security concerns are considered when all SLAs are set. This metric ensures that no risks creep in as new SLAs are set up or old ones re-negotiated. Justification: Whether a service is new or of long standing, its business requirements can be a pointer to possible security issues and these must be highlighted, along with proposed solutions to minimize them, in the SLA.
Audience:	Process Owner, IT Management, SLA Process Owner, Team Members, SIP Process Owner
Constraints:	None
Danger value:	70
Target value:	100
Possible values:	0-100%

Metric:	**Percentage of UCs (Underpinning Contracts) with explicit security specifications {%UCs}**
Description:	As with SLAs, the UCs ougth to be in the CMDB and their security clause can be compared to ensure that it is not just boilerplate.
Specification:	As with the above, all Underpinning Contracts ought, eventually, to comply with company security policy. This metric keeps a focus on this activity. Large risk can emerge from a badly negotiate UC.
Justification:	Underpinning Contracts must be considered actively to prevent security issues arising. This can be measured by this metric.
Audience:	Process Owner, IT Management, SLA Process Owner, Team Members, SIP Process Owner

Constraints:	UCs must be under document control.
Danger value:	75
Target value:	100
Possible values:	0-100%

Metric:	**Number of release security issues identified (back-outs/viruses etc.) {issues}**
Description:	All release plans must have a non-boilerplate entry for security issues.
Specification:	Release Management is a highly vulnerable entry point for security threats. An active control of release (particularly emergency releases) by Security Management will keep this metric properly low.
Justification:	Releases provide a high risk to security procedures. This ensures that there is an active external examination of the level of risk appropriate in each release planning document.
Audience:	Process Owner, IT Management, SLA Process Owner, Team Members, SIP Process Owner
Constraints:	Release documents must be under document control.
Danger value:	5
Target value:	0
Possible values:	999999

Metric:	**Number of changes backed out as a result of security issues {changes}**
Description:	This is measured by the closing disposition of changes - if they indicate security as a reason for back-out of a change then they count towards this metric.
Specification:	If changes introduce security issues then they are not being properly planned. A change turning up here ought to be fully investigated to ensure that it is not a result of a deliberate attack.
Justification:	Changes, including releases, must be planned and tested properly. If backouts occur as a result of security issues then there is a failure of control.
Audience:	Process Owner, IT Management, SLA Process Owner, Team Members, SIP Process Owner
Constraints:	None
Danger value:	5
Target value:	0
Possible values:	999999

Metric:	Security patch releasese speed {time}
Description:	All sorts of security patches and updates are released frequently.
Specification:	The time between the release of a security patch by a supplier and the implementation of it in the production environment.
Justification:	The time necessary for implementation of these security patches means vulnerability to a risk. The speedier the implementation the less vulnerability.
Audience:	Process Owner, IT Management, SLA Process Owner, Team Members, SIP Process Owner
Constraints:	Not receiving the security patches and or updates.
Danger value:	1 week
Target value:	2 days
Possible values:	Theoretically unlimited

N   Business Perspective metrics

The **goal** of **Business Perspective metrics** is **Quality of Experience** (QoE), a measure of business satisfaction aligned to business structures.

Mission Statement: To continually support and improve business effectiveness through the delivery of high quality IS services aligned and responsive to business needs, while maximizing the business return on investment in IS.

Process owner: IT Manager

The following three metrics are for the Business Perspective as a whole:

Metric Objective: Appropriate alignment of business and IT.

Metric:	Delivery cost per service {cost}
Description:	From the CMDB - how much each service costs. Service Calls * appropriate cost + Problem Management + fixed costs etc.
Specification:	This depends on Financial Management being in place, otherwise some proxy for cost will be required here (even Call Volume or Downtime per service could provide this). The calculation is simple (total cost)/(number of services). This example shows this as measured as a percentage of direct cost. That is the sum of incident, problem, change and operations devoted to a particular service divided by the total. This cost should decrease as service is improved - even though new services might show high cost during start up.
Justification:	This is a difficult measure (NOT SMART)! That does not mean that it is not a good goal of Financial Management to attempt to measure this as accurately as possible - to enable the Business Perspective to give a good picture of service costs to the Business.
Audience:	Process Owner, IT Management, SLA Process Owner, Business Customer, Team Members, SIP Process Owner
Constraints:	None
Danger value:	30
Target value:	20
Possible values:	0-100

Metric Objective: *To deliver effective IT/Business alignment.*

Metric:	**Customer Satisfaction {satisfaction}**
Description:	The overall sum of all Customer Satisfaction measures.
Specification:	Customer Satisfaction with IT Service Management.
Justification:	The Business Perspective is ultimately responsible for delivering effective business/IT alignment.
Audience:	Process Owner, IT Management, SLA Process Owner, Business Customer, Team Members, SIP Process Owner
Constraints:	None.
Danger value:	< 3
Target value:	4
Possible values:	0-5

Metric:	**Business Knowledge of IT {satisfaction}**
Description:	The level of satisfaction in the Business with the level of IT Business knowledge.
Specification:	Customer Satisfaction surveys to include a question of how satisfied the responder is with the level of knowledge of the Business shown by IT. This refers to knowledge level that the responder has found of his function when dealing with IT.
Justification:	All members of IT need to have some knowledge and awareness of the Business that they are providing services to. This metric measures the level of this knowledge. It is applied to the Business Perspective as effective Business/IT alignment requires that the Business trusts IT and that trust requires a level of mutual understanding and knowledge.
Audience:	Process Owner, IT Management, SLA Process Owner, Team Members, SIP Process Owner
Constraints:	None
Danger value:	< 3
Target value:	4
Possible values:	0-5

N.1 Business Relationship Management

Metric:	**Number of service complaints {complaints}**
Description:	The total number of complaints about the service reaching the organization.
Specification:	This gives an indication of the customer satisfaction, and of the quality of the organizations relationships.
Justification:	For good Relationship Management, an idea about the customer satisfaction is indispensable.
Audience:	Process Owner, IT Management, SLA Process Owner, Business Customer, Team Members, SIP Process Owner
Constraints:	Not everybody lets the organization know he's not satisfied.
Danger value:	20
Target value:	10
Possible values:	999999

Metric:	**Number of outstanding actions against last Service Review {actions}**
Description:	The number of actions, coming out of the last Service Review, that haven't been taken care of yet.
Specification:	This indicates how effective an organization handles its reviewing process and completes its action items.
Justification:	Effective processing of action items will increase customer satisfaction and thus improve business relationships.
Audience:	Process Owner, IT Management, SLA Process Owner, Business Customer, Team Members, SIP Process Owner
Constraints:	This only measures the speed, not the quality of the handling of the action items.
Danger value:	15
Target value:	10
Possible values:	999999

N.2 Supplier Relationship Management

Metric:	**Maximum incidents per supplier {incidents}**
Description:	Every incident will be traced back to a given supplier. The number of incidents per supplier will be counted.
Specification:	This is the number of incidents found to be caused, or partially caused, by the supplier with the most incidents. Good supplier management should drive this down. Incidents, rather than problems, are measured here, as the intention is to reduce business disruption.
Justification:	For good supplier management, it is important to know how satisfied you may be about his service.
Audience:	Process Owner, IT Management, SLA Process Owner, Team Members, SIP Process Owner

Constraints:	The metric doesn't account for the impact of the different incidents. It may very well be that a supplier causing only one, but very big, incident harms the business more than a supplier causing many, but small, incidents.
Danger value:	70
Target value:	50
Possible values:	999999

Metric:	**Percentage of contract suppliers conforming to standards {%suppliers}**
Description:	What part of your contract suppliers conforms to your standards.
Specification:	These are standards that are appropriate (ISO9000 or ISO20000). The aim is to achieve hundred percent of standards compliance with all suppliers. Once this is achieved, a more tactical quality measure can be substituted.
Justification:	The chance of an incident or problem will decrease when all parts of a system follow the same ways of working.
Audience:	Process Owner, IT Management, SLA Process Owner, Business Customer, Team Members, SIP Process Owner
Constraints:	Suppliers can conform to standards with their mouth, but measuring if they actually do in practice will be very difficult.
Danger value:	85
Target value:	95
Possible values:	0-100

Metric:	**Percentage of supplier reviews completed on time {%reviews}**
Description:	The Percentage of regularly scheduled reviews of suppliers that are completed on time.
Specification:	Review schedules that show reviews due in the past that have no completion summary or action points.
Justification:	Supplier reviews can seem unimportant when things are going well and can be let to slip. This is dangerous as it increases the risk that small issues can, left unattended, become serious problems.
Audience:	Process Owner, IT Management, SLA Process Owner, Team Members, SIP Process Owner
Constraints:	None
Danger value:	5
Target value:	2
Possible values:	0-100

Metric:	**Number of outstanding issues with suppliers {issues}**
Description:	Issues are raised either when they are discovered through incident or problem management or during supplier reviews. These are tracked by this metric.
Specification:	The count of the number of issues in the issue log.
Justification:	It is important that suppliers respond to issues raised in a timely manner.

Issues that remain outstanding will be visible through this metric and can enable work to manage them downwards. The danger is that, if this is not done, a list of outstanding issues can be seen by both parties as of lower importance than day to day operations which increases the risk that these issues, if not resolved, can lead to incidents.

Audience:	Process Owner, IT Management, SLA Process Owner, Team Members, SIP Process Owner
Constraints:	None
Danger value:	20
Target value:	10
Possible values:	0-100

N.3   Providing IT services

Mission Statement: *This falls under the Business Perspective. The service provider is responsible for providing IT services to the business, from the initial gathering of business requirements through application development, service deployment, day-to-day management, continuous improvement, and eventual retirement. For the business to view these services as being successful, they need to be of high quality, must meet changing businesss requirements, and be provided at an appropriate cost.*

Process owner: *Service Level Manager*

Metric Objective: *To supply business services with a minimum of disruption.*

Metric:	**Minimum Customer Satisfaction Score {satisfaction}**
Description:	The worst performing process.
Specification:	This is the minimum score found in all process metrics measured. The focus of Service Provision is to drive this up.
Justification:	Service Provision should be working to improve the least well performing process - probably through the SIP process. This identifies how well this is doing.
Audience:	Process Owner, IT Management, SLA Process Owner, Business Customer, Team Members, SIP Process Owner
Constraints:	None
Danger value:	< 3
Target value:	4
Possible values:	0-5

Metric:	**Number of incident {incidents}**
Description:	Ultimately this process should reduce the number of incidents over time. To avoid seasonal or other short-term events, this measure could be replaced with a rolling-average.
Specification:	The total number of incidents is a measure of the level of service disruption found by the organization.

Justification:	Incidents are the ultimate measure of service disruption.
Audience:	Process Owner, IT Management, SLA Process Owner, Business Customer, Team Members, SIP Process Owner
Constraints:	None
Danger value:	150
Target value:	100
Possible values:	9999999

Metric Objective: *Effective Service Delivery.*

Metric:	**Customer Satisfaction {satisfaction}**
Description:	This is a measure of delivery at the Business level.
Specification:	Overall Customer Satisfaction, as with Service Level Management.
Justification:	Effective service delivery is measured by Customer Satisfaction.
Audience:	Process Owner, IT Management, SLA Process Owner, Business Customer, Team Members, SIP Process Owner
Constraints:	None
Danger value:	< 3
Target value:	4
Possible values:	0-5

N.4   Planning, Review and Development

Mission Statement: *To ensure that IT processes have been planned effectively and that plans, once produced and approved, have been implemented correctly.*

Process owner: *Project Office.*

Metric Objective: *Review plans and make effective changes in line with business requirements.*

Metric:	**Number of issues identified in final Plan Review {issues}**
Description:	Simple issue count.
Specification:	The number of issues shown in the review.
Justification:	This gives a measure of how much change is required to the document - over time, as processes improve, the number of changes required at review should reduce.
Audience:	Process Owner, IT Management, SLA Process Owner, Team Members, SIP Process Owner
Constraints:	None
Danger value:	8
Target value:	6
Possible values:	999999

Metric:	**Number of plans signed off for implementation {plans}**
Description:	This is a count of activity, but also of authorization. Though this does not measure the complexity of the plans, it is a measure of the number. Though it would make this a more complex metric, the predicted scope of the project in man-days could be taken as the count, rather than simply counting each plan as one count.
Specification:	Since documentation will be kept in the CMDB, the status can be measured directly. Plans that move to the signed-off status will be counted.
Justification:	Plans must not only be produced, but also authorized.
Audience:	Process Owner, IT Management, SLA Process Owner, Team Members, SIP Process Owner
Constraints:	None
Danger value:	2
Target value:	4
Possible values:	999999

N.5 Liaison, Education and Communication

Mission Statement: *Ensure that IT, users and customers are aware of current and future plans as they affect them and are encouraged to contribute their ideas for improvement.*

Process owner: *Project Office*

Metric Objective: *To have suitably qualified staff in all positions.*

Metric:	**Number of late actions in Communications Plan {actions}**
Description:	All actions in the Communications Plan should have a target date. This measures the number of actions that are over date.
Specification:	Actions not completed by date of metric measure.
Justification:	Actions identified need to be followed-up. This shows how effectively this is being done.
Audience:	Process Owner, IT Management, SLA Process Owner, Team Members, SIP Process Owner
Constraints:	None
Danger value:	5
Target value:	3
Possible values:	999999

Metric:	**Percentage of IT staff not at optimal training level for their position {%staff}**
Description:	Either from HR, or from an IT training and competence DB, the level of appropriate education and experience in the organization.
Specification:	A measurement of staff competencies.
Justification:	ISO20000 requires that staff can be shown to have appropriate training and experience for their positions.
Audience:	Process Owner, IT Management, SLA Process Owner, Team Members, SIP Process Owner
Constraints:	None
Danger value:	2
Target value:	1
Possible values:	0-100

O Metrics for Continuous Service Improvement Programmes (SIP)

Mission Statement: *Run the SIP as an on-going programme. Communicate with IT Management to ensure that all processes are subject to specific SIP attention at least every two years. Ensure that the process most in need of attention, as shown by the results of process metrics, is scheduled for action in a timely manner.*

Process owner: *Project Office*

Metric Objective: *To improve current process operation in line with business requirements.*

Metric:	**Overall Customer Satisfaction {satisfaction}**
Description:	The mean of all Customer Satisfaction measures.
Specification:	This is the overall satisfaction of end-customers. Ultimately the SIP should be delivering improved Customer Satisfaction to end customers as well as reduction in cost.
Justification:	Over time the SIP should drive up Customer Satisfaction.
Audience:	Process Owner, IT Management, SLA Process Owner, Business Customer, Team Members, SIP Process Owner
Constraints:	None
Danger value:	< 3
Target value:	4
Possible values:	0-5

Metric:	**Percentage of cost saving in last process SIP {%saving}**
Description:	How much the SIP has reduced overall IT costs.
Specification:	Usually each process is, in turn, given the full attention of the SIP. Once this is complete, a measurable cost saving ought to be the result. How exactly to measure this will depend on the process and be defined by the SIP. This can then be measured until the next process has completed the SIP. This ensures that unexpected negative consequences of the SIP can be caught early and the genuine contribution of the SIP made visible.
Justification:	The SIP improvement must have tangible results and cost saving will be measurable and tangible.
Audience:	Process Owner, IT Management, SLA Process Owner, Business Customer, Team Members, SIP Process Owner
Constraints:	Financial Management needs to be in place for this to be accurate.
Danger value:	5
Target value:	10
Possible values:	0-100

Metric:	**Percentage of processes overdue for SIP {%processes}**
Description:	If any process is overdue for SIP attention.
Specification:	If ten core ITIL processes go through the SIP process every ten months (that is one process a month), then over due would mean that one process is eleven or more months from the last improvement.
Justification:	Though the SIP concentrates firstly on processes that are shown, by their metrics, to be in need of improvement, all processes must be examined periodically.
Audience:	Process Owner, IT Management, SLA Process Owner, Business Customer, Team Members, SIP Process Owner
Constraints:	None
Danger value:	20
Target value:	10
Possible values:	0-100

Metric:	**Number of outstanding approved actions that have not achieved their objective {actions}**
Description:	Actions not successful.
Specification:	All actions that come out of the SIP are documented and their intended improvement target agreed. When these actions have been approved, this metric will track their implementation. A SIP will not be successful if the actions recommended do not take place!
Justification:	Actions recommended by the SIP must be SMART. That means that we can monitor their effect. It is important that they do achieve the improvements that are expected. This metric measures if they do.
Audience:	Process Owner, IT Management, SLA Process Owner, Business Customer, Team Members, SIP Process Owner
Constraints:	None
Danger value:	5
Target value:	3
Possible values:	999999

Metric:	**Number of outstanding actions in SIP Communications Plan {actions}**
Description:	This establishes that there is a communications plan for the SIP and that the actions in it take place on time.
Specification:	Improvements made by the SIP must be measured, reported and communicated - this communication is through the Communications Plan and this item measures any slippage in the communication. This also ensures that the measurement and reporting is complete too.
Justification:	The SIP Communications Plan actions are important to the success of the plan - hence this metric to monitor them.
Audience:	Process Owner, IT Management, SLA Process Owner, Business Customer, Team Members, SIP Process Owner
Constraints:	None
Danger value:	10

Target value:	5
Possible values:	999999

Metric:	**Number of approved revisions to Service Management policies, plans and procedures {revisions}**
Description:	Changes to the SIP.
Specification:	It is not necessary that there are lots of changes and only changes that are actually approved are relevant. However, the SIP needs to take a holistic view and this metric ensures that these revisions are understood to be within the scope of the SIP if necessary.
Justification:	This makes the changes from the SIP visible - particularly those to policies and procedures. It is important that these are understood to be part of the scope of the SIP.
Audience:	Process Owner, IT Management, SLA Process Owner, Business Customer, Team Members, SIP Process Owner
Constraints:	The SIP must be under document control.
Danger value:	2
Target value:	5
Possible values:	999999

Metric:	**Number of improvements carried out by process owners - outside SIP cycle {improvements}**
Description:	Improvements made by process owners.
Specification:	The SIP is the on-going engine of Service Improvement. However, each process owner has a responsibility to try to improve his process. These improvements must be coordinated through the SIP process and reported through this metric so that all cost savings can be properly evaluated.
Justification:	There is a danger that the SIP is seen as the only means to improve processes. Process owners have a responsibility to take action to improve their processes as well. This recognizes this work and ensures that it is taking place.
Audience:	Process Owner, IT Management, SLA Process Owner, Business Customer, Team Members, SIP Process Owner
Constraints:	None
Danger value:	2
Target value:	5
Possible values:	9999999

Metric:	**Number of SIPs on Target {SIPs}**
Description:	Service Improvement Plans that are on target.
Specification:	SIPs that have action items due in the past.
Justification:	The SIP is a fundamental part of the major job of delivering Services of appropriate quality to the Customer. If actions are defined in any SIP it is crucial that they are acted upon according to the plan. This identifies any slippages. Clearly there may be good reasons for these, but the fact that there is any slippage must be visible otherwise many other metrics that rely upon the SIP for their improvement may be adversely affected as well.

Audience:	Process Owner, IT Management, SLA Process Owner, Business Customer, Team Members, SIP Process Owner
Constraints:	None
Danger value:	2
Target value:	2
Possible values:	9999999

Metric Objective: *To provide measurable improvement to processes.*

Metric:	**Percentage of overall improvement since last benchmark {%improvement}**
Description:	Improvement measured by the results of the process metrics taken as a three month rolling average.
Specification:	Relevant input must be gathered from all the processes. It is important that the contributions of all the process owners are recognized and measured.
Justification:	Annual benchmarks of process metrics can be taken so that the processes can be measured against these. Those processes that have been through a SIP improvement ought to show their metrics to have improved.
Audience:	Process Owner, IT Management, SLA Process Owner, Business Customer, Team Members, SIP Process Owner
Constraints:	Metrics must be the same as when the benchmark was taken for this to be meaningful.
Danger value:	3
Target value:	5
Possible values:	0-100

Metric Objective: *To make effective improvements to Service Management processes.*

Metric:	**Number of recommendations for improvement received from other process owners {recommendations}**
Description:	Processes that have interfaces to a process undergoing the SIP ought to have recommendations to make. These are measured by this.
Specification:	This is a measure of activity. Is the SIP producing genuine changes?
Justification:	The SIP is not an externally imposed audit. It takes information from process metrics and advice from other process owners. It is important that other process owners provide this.
Audience:	Process Owner, IT Management, SLA Process Owner, Business Customer, Team Members, SIP Process Owner
Constraints:	Process owner recommendations must be under document control.
Danger value:	3
Target value:	5
Possible values:	999999

Metric:	**Number of changes requested for process improvement {changes}**
Description:	Changes requested to improve processes.
Specification:	RFCs generated by the SIP process.
Justification:	Changes to processes must be made through Change Management. So the count of RFCs is a measure of how active the SIP process has been and how much change is required by the processes under review.
Audience:	Process Owner, IT Management, SLA Process Owner, Business Customer, Team Members, SIP Process Owner
Constraints:	None
Danger value:	3
Target value:	5
Possible values:	999999

P   Risk Management metrics

Mission Statement: *Risk management in ITIL is owned by the Availability Management process - though a number of other areas use Risk Management as well. The metrics for this process do not include Customer Satisfaction because this is already part of the Availability Management metrics.*

Process owner: *Availability Manager*

Metric Objective: *Risk management in ITIL is owned by the Availability Management process - though a number of other areas use Risk Management as well.*

Metric:	**Percentage of CIs covered by Business Impact Analysis {%CIs}**
Description:	Is BIA complete?
Specification:	The Business Impact Analysis will consider classes of CI - not necessarily every one! Ideally, all CIs ought to have a link to an appropriate BIA. The metrics for this process do not include Customer Satisfaction because this is already part of the Availability Management metrics.
Justification:	All CIs ought to have been included in a BIA at some time - and marked to this effect.
Audience:	Process Owner, IT Management, SLA Process Owner, Team Members, SIP Process Owner
Constraints:	None
Danger value:	60
Target value:	75
Possible values:	0-100

Metric Objective: *IT Service Continuity Management plans to reduce the business impact of all foreseeable risks.*

Metric:	**Percentage of BIA documents not reviewed within required time. {%documents}**
Description:	An annual review of all Business Impact Analysis would be required for most businesses - more frequent if volatile. Whatever has been agreed as an appropriate review period must be logged and kept under document control to statisfy this metric.
Specification:	This is a measure of document reviews to check that Business Impact Analysis is reviewed when specified.
Justification:	If Business Impact Analysis only occurs occasionally or sporadically, it is possible for changes in the environment to occur that can increase (or decrease) previously established impacts of various scenarios. This means either that exposure is higher than believed or, possibly, that expensive risk reduction actions are in place unnecessarily.

Audience:	Process Owner, IT Management, SLA Process Owner, Team Members, SIP Process Owner
Constraints:	None
Danger value:	12
Target value:	20
Possible values:	0-100

Metric:	**Percentage of processes subject to Operational Risk Assessment (ORA) {%processes}**
Description:	It might be useful to conduct the ORA as part of the SIP process. It is important that it has taken place at least annually. To measure these risks, each incident has to include a section for listing operational risk revealed by the incident.
Specification:	All processes are subject to operational risk. This metric lists those where this risk can be demonstrated by incidents that have occurred that indicate that the process is at risk.
Justification:	This helps give a picture of how incidents map to operational risk and which processes appear to be at greatest risk.
Audience:	Process Owner, IT Management, SLA Process Owner, Team Members, SIP Process Owner
Constraints:	None
Danger value:	20
Target value:	12
Possible values:	0-100

> **Metric Objective:** IT Service Continuity Management plans to reduce the impact of all foreseeable risks.

Metric:	**Number of incidents relating to risks not in ORA {incidents}**
Description:	The Operational Risk Assessment (ORA) must be as accurate as possible. This metric measures how inaccurate it is - each event measured here has a potential to produce a large impact on the organization and is also one that has not been predicted, forecast or imagined.
Specification:	These will be recognized and reported as such by Problem Management. If, for example, a software release has been installed without being subject to ORA, then incidents relating to that release are unconsidered risks. To measure this it will be necessary to link CIs to their corresponding ORA.
Justification:	It is important to understand how accurate the ORA actually is. It is never possible to account for all risks, but the occurrence of events that are not considered in it shows where the process of risk identification can be improved.
Audience:	Process Owner, IT Management, SLA Process Owner, Team Members, SIP Process Owner
Constraints:	None
Danger value:	20

Target value:	10
Possible values:	999999

Metric:	**Percentage of incidents where occurrence is higher than predicted in ORA {%incidents}**
Description:	The ORA predicts a probability of High/Medium/Low for the risk to CIs. If this is shown to be wrong consistently then the ORA must be updated in line with the actual risk.
Specification:	This metric requires that a quantitative definition for High (say > 200 events/month), Medium (100 - 200) and Low (<100) is defined. This measures how the forecast risk matches the actual occurrence.
Justification:	Forecasts are inaccurate by nature. It is important that they are made, however, and are kept as accurate as possible for business needs. This metric ensures that forecasts are compared to actual events to detect deviations so that forecasts can be made more accurate.
Audience:	Process Owner, IT Management, SLA Process Owner, Team Members, SIP Process Owner
Constraints:	None
Danger value:	70
Target value:	50
Possible values:	0-100

Metric:	**Percentage of CIs where downtime is greater than predicted in ORA {%CIs}**
Description:	The forecast business impact of particular risks can be compared to the actual occurence of these risks so that forecasts can be improved. This is only possible, and appropriate, for fairly common low-level risks.
Specification:	Using the linkage mentioned above, the predicted impact of an outage to a particular CI on the business can be calculated and compared to the actual downtime experienced by the business
Justification:	The forecasting of business impact is important in deciding what resources ought to be provided to reduce a particular risk. If the forecasts are inaccurate the business may be exposed to a higher level of risk than it believes is the case. This metric ensures that impact is measured against forecast allowing forecasts to be improved.
Audience:	Process Owner, IT Management, SLA Process Owner, Team Members, SIP Process Owner
Constraints:	This is not possible and will not improve the quality of forecasting of large, unusual risks and their impact. The measurement of the impact of small risks can help, however, with the extrapolation of such impacts.
Danger value:	70
Target value:	50
Possible values:	0-100

Metric:	**Number of actions to reduce risk {actions}**
Description:	The process of documenting actions taken in response to indentified risks must be under document control so that these actions can automatically be identified.
Specification:	In reaction to discrepancies shown above (or as part of the SIP), action needs to be taken to reduce particular risks. This measures documented actions.
Justification:	New risks must not only be identified, but actions to minimize the impact or reduce them must also be taken. This measures this activity - taken along with the measure of new risks identified, this ensures that risks are not simply identified, but that there are also actions taken to manage them.
Audience:	Process Owner, IT Management, SLA Process Owner, Team Members, SIP Process Owner
Constraints:	No
Danger value:	3
Target value:	5
Possible values:	999999

Metric Objective: *IT Service Continuity minimizes the likely risk of all foreseeable risks.*

Metric:	**Number of newly identified risks {risks}**
Description:	New risks that are documented under document control.
Specification:	Risks change over time, particularly business risks. IT risk assessment must have an up-to-date picture of what the current risk is. Regular identification of new risks both internal and external is important.
Justification:	New risks are identified and then their impact to the business is analysed and possible counter-measures implemented. If the risks are not identified in the first place then the latter cannot happen. This ensures that an active consideration of possible risk is a regular part of IT thinking.
Audience:	Process Owner, IT Management, SLA Process Owner, Team Members, SIP Process Owner
Constraints:	No
Danger value:	2
Target value:	3
Possible values:	999999

Metric Objective: *All CIs are included in the IT Service Continuity Plan.*

Metric:	**Percentage of CIs not covered by Service Continuity Plan {%CIs}**
Description:	All CIs should be covered by the Service Continuity Plan. They might be 'no action' items, but this must be explicit in the plan. All new services

	must have appropriate entries in the Service Continuity Plan.
Specification:	A verification that all CIs are linked to the Service Continuity Plan - that is they are taken into account, even if as no action items.
Justification:	If CIs do not appear in the Service Continuity Plan then they cannot be catered for in it so they are at a high risk because they will not be recovered in the case of a disaster. This metric ensures that new CIs are dynamically added to the plan in the appropriate section preventing this risk.
Audience:	Process Owner, IT Management, SLA Process Owner, Team Members, SIP Process Owner
Constraints:	No
Danger value:	10
Target value:	5
Possible values:	0-100

Metric Objective: *To ensure that services are delivered to the business in line with agreed service levels - through internal and external suppliers.*

Metric:	**Number of meetings with suppliers, and internal process owners {meetings}**
Description:	Meetings with partners may not achieve anything. However, if meetings are not taking place then supplier, and internal, attention to Risk Management may reduce. Once this is a regular activity, it might be more appropriate to measure actions achieved as a result of the meetings.
Specification:	Measured by the recording of minutes of meetings with suppliers and process owners as kept under document control.
Justification:	Since meeting agendas and minutes are kept under document control, it is possible to ensure that they are taking place. It would be ideal to measure that they are also meeting their objectives, but this is not so easy to achieve. The job described in 'The Business Perspective' Part I involves a high level of communication with suppliers for various reasons. If this job is to be measured, some measure of how well this communication is going (apart from simply 'supplier satisfaction') is required. That is why this is here. There should be a fixed process for regular supplier meetings, with basic standard agenda to cover matters likely to cause problems. This metric needs to ensure that these meetings are taking place so that an active communcation link is in place - rather than a fire-fighting or end-of-contract driven process which tends to be the problem today.
Audience:	Process Owner, IT Management, SLA Process Owner, Team Members, SIP Process Owner
Constraints:	None
Danger value:	1
Target value:	3
Possible values:	999999

Q Documentation Management metrics

> **Mission Statement:** *Keep documentation control standards and measure compliance. Make sure that documents are secure but well indexed so as to be easy to access by those authorized. Maintain an historical audit trail and verify that all relevant documents are managed under IT service continuity plan so as to be available in the case of a disaster.*

> **Process owner:** *Configuration Management*

> **Metric Objective:** *To have documents following the appropriate document management policy.*

Metric:	**Percentage of documents late for planned revision {%documents}**
Description:	Documents that are out of date because planned revisions have not taken place.
Specification:	Documents with revision dates before today.
Justification:	If documents are not revised when agreed then plans based on these documents will also be out of date and my cause service outages.
Audience:	Process Owner, IT Management, SLA Process Owner, Team Members, SIP Process Owner
Constraints:	None
Danger value:	5
Target value:	3
Possible values:	0-100

Metric:	**Percentage of documents not reviewed for one year {%documents}**
Description:	Have documents had their annual review?
Specification:	This is set to one year as a general case, but will be the time, according to document management policy during which documents ought to be reviewed.
Justification:	All documents ought to be reviewed and either changed, marked as adequate or deleted in light of whether they are still current.
Audience:	Process Owner, IT Management, SLA Process Owner, Team Members, SIP Process Owner
Constraints:	None
Danger value:	5
Target value:	3
Possible values:	0-100

Metric:	**Percentage of documents not accessed for one year {%documents}**
Description:	Documents unused for a long period.
Specification:	Documents that are not used.
Justification:	The exact period will depend on the Document Management Policy, but documents that are not used must be reviewed for deletion or relevance.
Audience:	Process Owner, IT Management, SLA Process Owner, Team Members, SIP Process Owner
Constraints:	None
Danger value:	15
Target value:	10
Possible values:	0-100

Metric:	**Number of outstanding requests for document changes {requests}**
Description:	Those documents with unsatisfied change requests.
Specification:	Document change requests not honoured.
Justification:	Secure documents or those with restricted access will have requests for change lodged against them - these must be actioned appropriately. This is a measure of how well that process is working.
Audience:	Process Owner, IT Management, SLA Process Owner, Team Members, SIP Process Owner
Constraints:	None
Danger value:	10
Target value:	5
Possible values:	999999

Metric:	**Number of documents not removed after end of life {documents}**
Description:	Documents still existing that ought to have been deleted.
Specification:	Documents on the system after their delete-by date.
Justification:	Document policy, following legal and security issues determines the length of life of verious documents.
Audience:	Process Owner, IT Management, SLA Process Owner, Team Members, SIP Process Owner
Constraints:	None
Danger value:	10
Target value:	5
Possible values:	999999

Metric:	**Number of SLAs missing documentation {SLAs}**
Description:	SLAs should comply with requirements as defined in the policy.
Specification:	SLAs lacking proper supporting documentation.
Justification:	The SLA documentation requirements must be carefully defined to ensure that adequate information is included - this checks that this has been followed in all SLAs.

Audience:	Process Owner, IT Management, SLA Process Owner, Business Customer, Team Members, SIP Process Owner
Constraints:	None
Danger value:	5
Target value:	2
Possible values:	999999

Metric:	**Number of incomplete Service Management policies and plans {plans/policies}**
Description:	Plans that are missing required sections or signatures.
Specification:	These documents must follow standard templates so that missing sections or signatures can be measured.
Justification:	Where plans have a consistent structure (like SLAs) this must be adhered to.
Audience:	Process Owner, IT Management, SLA Process Owner, Team Members, SIP Process Owner
Constraints:	None
Danger value:	5
Target value:	2
Possible values:	999999

Metric:	**Number of incompatibilities between specific plans and the service management plan {incompatibilities}**
Description:	Manual cross checking will be required of specific plans according to a roster if centralized sheduling cannot achieve this.
Specification:	Plans must be consistent and follow policy - this checks for inconsistencies.
Justification:	Plans must be consistent to be effective.
Audience:	Process Owner, IT Management, SLA Process Owner, Team Members, SIP Process Owner
Constraints:	None
Danger value:	10
Target value:	5
Possible values:	999999

Metric Objective: *To have secure documents that support other processes where appropriate.*

Metric:	**Number of documentation related incidents {incidents}**
Description:	This is based on the closing disposition of incident and call records.
Specification:	Incidents that have a closing code that relates them to documentation errors.
Justification:	Documentation management must work to ensure that incidents are not caused by errors or misleading documentation.

Audience:	Process Owner, IT Management, SLA Process Owner, Team Members, SIP Process Owner
Constraints:	None
Danger value:	40
Target value:	20
Possible values:	999999

Metric Objective: *That Document Management processes are delivered effectively.*

Metric:	**Customer Satisfaction {satisfaction}**
Description:	Customer Satisfaction as measured by the process(es) most closely associated with this one.
Specification:	Customer Satisfaction metric as described in the Process Relationship diagram.
Justification:	This is a subjective, but genuine, measure of the quality of the output of a process.
Audience:	Process Owner, IT Management, SLA Process Owner, Team Members, SIP Process Owner
Constraints:	No
Danger value:	< 3
Target value:	4
Possible values:	0-5

R   Metrics for Competence, Awareness and Training (CAT)

> **Mission Statement:** *Ensure that target levels of training and competence are reached and maintained in the organization to the level required by ISO20000.*

> **Process owner:** *Service Level Management*

> **Metric Objective:** *To have suitably qualified staff in all positions.*

Metric:	**Number of late actions from Awareness Campaign {actions}**
Description:	Outstanding actions.
Specification:	Actions dated and not completed before the measure of this metric.
Justification:	This checks that the awareness campaign is taking place according to plan.
Audience:	Process Owner, IT Management, SLA Process Owner, Team Members, SIP Process Owner
Constraints:	Actions must be under document control.
Danger value:	10
Target value:	5
Possible values:	999999

Metric:	**Number of job descriptions missing specific competence requirement {job descriptions}**
Description:	Job descriptions held in HR or on the CMDB attached to organizational positions can be linked to Skills Framework for the Information Age (SFIA). qualifications - where these links are lacking we have the measure. Specification: Required competences might be derived from the SFIA.
Justification:	ISO20000 requires the demonstration of staff competencies for particular positions.
Audience:	Process Owner, IT Management, SLA Process Owner, HR, Team Members, SIP Process Owner
Constraints:	None
Danger value:	5
Target value:	2
Possible values:	999999

Metric:	**Percentage of IT staff with professional industry recognition {%staff}**
Description:	This information can be found in an appropriate skills matrix that includes training and experience.
Specification:	This is a Project Management, Service Management, Computer Science or other recognized body - a Member of the BCS, Fellow of the ISM or similar.
Justification:	Senior staff experience can be shown by such membership of recognized bodies.
Audience:	Process Owner, IT Management, SLA Process Owner, Team Members, SIP P O
Process Constraints:	Owner None
Danger value:	5
Target value:	10
Possible values:	0-100

Metric:	**Mean Percentage of shortfall from optimal level of training {%courses}**
Description:	This information is to be supplied by a skills matrix.
Specification:	For each member of IT, that ought to have completed N training courses, but has, in fact, completed M training courses, this is N-M/N * 100 - with this metric being the mean.
Justification:	This gives a rough measure of the shortfall. Suitable training plans can improve this over time as long as attrition is not too high.
Audience:	Process Owner, IT Management, SLA Process Owner, HR, Team Members, SIP Process Owner
Constraints:	This does not take into account those who are over- qualified, as they do not make up for people who are not adequately qualified!
Danger value:	10
Target value:	5
Possible values:	0-100

Metric:	**Percentage of staff with a signed Personal Development Plan {%staff}**
Description:	Development plans properly approved.
Specification:	All staff should have an up-to-date signed personal development plan - these should be kept in the CMDB so as to measure this metric.
Justification:	Development plans ensure that staff keep abreast of latest developments, they keep competence levels high and reduced atrittion.
Audience:	Process Owner, IT Management, SLA Process Owner, Business Customer, Team Members, SIP Process Owner
Constraints:	None
Danger value:	90
Target value:	95
Possible values:	999999

Metric:	**Percentage of staff with no defined role or responsibility {%staff}**
Description:	Staff who are not linked to defined roles and responsibilities.
Specification:	Roles and responsibilities defined at the organizational level link to staff who hold them. This metric lists staff who are not linked to any defined roles or responsibilities.
Justification:	When people join or change function, defining a formal role with formal responsibilities according to those defined can seem like a minor administrative detail. This metric ensures that it is kept visible. If people do not have these defined then they can't be measured against them and are in a position where they can't be sure if they are performing properly. This is unfair and can lead to operational inefficiencies.
Audience:	Process Owner, IT Management, SLA Process Owner, HR, Team Members, SIP Process Owner
Constraints:	None
Danger value:	3
Target value:	2
Possible values:	999999

Metric Objective: To have suitably trained staff for all positions.

Metric:	**Percentage of IT staff not at optimal training level for their position {%staff}**
Description:	If training levels, training plans and training histories are kept in the CMDB then this can be determined from those.
Specification:	To measure this, the optimal training level must be defined for all IT positions and a training plan for each individual kept that can measure whether the training is optimal or not.
Justification:	ISO20000 requires suitably qualified staff.
Audience:	Process Owner, IT Management, SLA Process Owner, Team Members, SIP Process Owner
Constraints:	None
Danger value:	85
Target value:	95
Possible values:	0-100

Metric Objective: *To have suitably trained staff.*

Metric:	**Percentage of staff not meeting minimum competence {%staff}**
Description:	Information from a skills matrix.
Specification:	This is related to the level of training, but can be improved by recruiting appropriately qualified staff.
Justification:	People not trained for their jobs are a risk to the business.
Audience:	Process Owner, IT Management, SLA Process Owner, Team Members, SIP Process Owner
Constraints:	None
Danger value:	5
Target value:	10
Possible values:	0-100

Metric Objective: *To ensure suitably trained staff.*

Metric:	**Percentage of staff with overdue actions against their development plan {%staff}**
Description:	Outstanding actions against development plans.
Specification:	These actions to be kept in the CMDB so that they can be measured for this metric.
Justification:	This ensures that actions agreed in development plans actually materialize which improves staff morale.
Audience:	Process Owner, IT Management, SLA Process Owner, Team Members, SIP Process Owner
Constraints:	None
Danger value:	15
Target value:	10
Possible values:	999999

Metric Objective: *To maintain high levels of awareness of IT projects and achievements in the organization.*

Metric:	**Percentage of awareness in organization {%awareness}**
Description:	Awareness as shown by polls and Service Desk scripts.
Specification:	This is measured by regular sample polls and by questions to callers to the Service Desk. If an awareness campaign is in progress, questions related to it can be asked when closing an incident and the measure of the percentage of users who are aware of the nature of the campaign measured. This can be used to improve the effectiveness of campaigns.
Justification:	IT must communicate effectively with the organization, this establishes the effectiveness of the communication.
Audience:	Process Owner, IT Management, SLA Process Owner, Team Members, SIP Process Owner

Constraints:	None
Danger value:	70
Target value:	80
Possible values:	0-100

Metric Objective: *To ensure that adequate levels of staff competence are kept.*

Metric:	**Percentage of IT staff turnover {%staff}**
Description:	How many staff leave or are hired in a year.
Specification:	Measured by personnel or NT login turnover.
Justification:	High levels of staff turn-over tend to mean poor morale and poor levels of retaining competent staff.
Audience:	Process Owner, IT Management, SLA Process Owner, Team Members, SIP Process Owner
Constraints:	None
Danger value:	10
Target value:	5
Possible values:	999999

Metric Objective: *To have adequate resourcing level.*

Metric:	**Number of outstanding job requisitions {requisitions}**
Description:	Measured by HR job requisitions for IT staff.
Specification:	New staff, no matter how well qualified, are not familiar with the organization. Such a high level of staff turnover, even of well-qualified staff, indicates a low level of competence in the organization. This is a measure of the difficulty of recruitment of adequately qualified staff. The requisitions might be outstanding because management has not approved the expenditure or because a suitable candidate cannot be found. In either case, the organization is short of that particular employee, so the level of desired competence is below what it ought to be.
Justification:	If these remain high it shows either high turnover or low recruitment.
Audience:	Process Owner, IT Management, SLA Process Owner, Team Members, SIP Process Owner
Constraints:	None
Danger value:	7
Target value:	4
Possible values:	999999

S   Metrics for Programme and Project Management

Mission Statement: Deliver projects and run Programmes to the required standards, by use of Prince2 or similar project method standard.

Process owner: Project Office

Metric Objective: To follow appropriate project and programme standards of delivery.

Metric:	**Number of milestones missed {milestone}**
Description:	Milestones are measured in the documentation store - CMDB.
Specification:	A count of milestones missed this month.
Justification:	This checks that the detail of project management policy is being adhered to.
Audience:	Process Owner, IT Management, SLA Process Owner, Team Members, SIP Process Owner
Constraints:	Documents must follow document storage policy.
Danger value:	1
Target value:	2
Possible values:	999999

Metric:	**Total project delay this month {time}**
Description:	This is measured from project documents found in the CMDB/Document store.
Specification:	A count of the number of days the project has slipped - measured by the days that milestones have slipped this month.
Justification:	Project information must be available to understand future change and availability requirements.
Audience:	Process Owner, IT Management, SLA Process Owner, Team Members, SIP Process Owner
Constraints:	None
Danger value:	5
Target value:	2
Possible values:	999999

Metric:	**Number of new project issues {issues}**
Description:	Project issue list.
Specification:	This is the number of new issues raised in the project this month. The increase in size of the issue list.
Justification:	All projects have issue lists - they do need to be managed and to be manageable. This follows their progress over time to makes sure that they are.

Audience:	Process Owner, IT Management, SLA Process Owner, Team Members, SIP Process Owner
Constraints:	None
Danger value:	5
Target value:	2
Possible values:	999999

Metric:	**Number of project issues resolved this month {issues}**
Description:	Issues resolved in the last period.
Specification:	This is the decrease in the size of the issue list.
Justification:	This shows positive resolution of issues and is a sign of a well managed project if high.
Audience:	Process Owner, IT Management, SLA Process Owner, Team Members, SIP Process Owner
Constraints:	None
Danger value:	2
Target value:	5
Possible values:	999999

Metric:	**Number of risks identified {risks}**
Description:	If this is growing fast it is an early warning of project difficulties ahead.
Specification:	The risk list for this month.
Justification:	The earlier the warning of problems the easier it is to resolve them in good time.
Audience:	Process Owner, IT Management, SLA Process Owner, Team Members, SIP Process Owner
Constraints:	None
Danger value:	10
Target value:	6
Possible values:	999999

Metric:	**Critical Path delay {time}**
Description:	A measure of genuine delay to projects.
Specification:	The cumulative delay of any sub-projects on the identified critical path in days.
Justification:	This requires that the critical path is properly identified and documented (already a good thing) and that delays on it can be objectively measured.
Audience:	Process Owner, IT Management, SLA Process Owner, Team Members, SIP Process Owner
Constraints:	None
Danger value:	4
Target value:	2
Possible values:	999999

Metric:	**Escalation {issues}**
Description:	How difficult is the current environment.
Specification:	The number of issues/risks that have been escalated by the project manager.
Justification:	Escalations of appropriate issues are to be welcomed - and need to be measured. To get an idea of the risks faced by current projects.
Audience:	Process Owner, IT Management, SLA Process Owner, Team Members, SIP Process Owner
Constraints:	None
Danger value:	5
Target value:	1
Possible values:	999999

Metric:	**Number of project meetings slipped {meetings}**
Description:	Measured from the document store.
Specification:	The number of project meetings that have slipped by more than 1 day this month.
Justification:	This is usually a minor issue, but repeated slippage is a sign that a project is under-resourced or under too much pressure.
Audience:	Process Owner, IT Management, SLA Process Owner, Team Members, SIP Process Owner
Constraints:	None
Danger value:	4
Target value:	2
Possible values:	999999

Metric:	**Estimated percentage of certainty of meeting project end-date on budget {%probability}**
Description:	Documented forecasts from the document store.
Specification:	How certain the project manager is that the project will end on time and on budget.
Justification:	These forecasts are important to check the quality of project delivery as well as for Capacity Management planning.
Audience:	Process Owner, IT Management, SLA Process Owner, Business Customer, Team Members, SIP Process Owner
Constraints:	None
Danger value:	70
Target value:	80
Possible values:	0-100

Metric:	**Number of outstanding actions from steering meetings {actions}**
Description:	Actions agreed to at steering meetings that are not complete after their agreed completion date.
Specification:	Actions with a completion date in the past and a status other than 'closed' Justification: If projects are running into trouble or out of resources, one of the first signs is that actions are agreed to, but then not completed on time. This metric enables the warning sign to be picked up early.
Audience:	Process Owner, IT Management, SLA Process Owner, Team Members, SIP Process Owner
Constraints:	None
Danger value:	10
Target value:	5
Possible values:	999999

Metric Objective: *That Service Management processes are delivered effectively.*

Metric:	**Customer Satisfaction {satisfaction}**
Description:	This is measured at project review time, though comments related to projects received by the Service Desk ought to be included in the measure.
Specification:	Customer Satisfaction with all projects and programmes delivered.
Justification:	Projects must be delivered so as to satisfy the users and customers.
Audience:	Process Owner, IT Management, SLA Process Owner, Business Customer, Team Members, SIP Process Owner
Constraints:	None
Danger value:	< 3
Target value:	4
Possible values:	0-5